Visual Analytics with SAS® Viya®

Special Collection

Foreword by
Rob Collum

sas.com/books

Table of Contents

Free SAS® e-Books: Special Collection

In this series, we have carefully curated a collection of papers that introduces and provides context to the various areas of analytics. Topics covered illustrate the power of SAS solutions that are available as tools for data analysis, highlighting a variety of commonly used techniques.

Discover more free SAS e-books!
support.sas.com/freesasebooks

sas.com/books
for additional books and resources.

THE POWER TO KNOW®

About This Book

What Does This Collection Cover?

SAS® Visual Analytics is a business intelligence and analytics platform that provides visual exploration and discovery, self-service analytics, and interactive reporting for organizations of all sizes. All organizations have a wide variety of users, and each user needs something different from data and analytics. SAS Visual Analytics allows everyone to easily discover and share powerful insights that inspire action.

The papers included in this special collection demonstrate the wide-ranging capabilities and applications of visual analytics across several industries. They are excerpts from the SAS Global Users Group *Proceedings*. For more SAS Global Forum *Proceedings,* visit the online versions of the Proceedings.

More helpful resources are available at support.sas.com and sas.com/books.

We Want to Hear from You

Do you have questions about a SAS Press book that you are reading? Contact us at saspress@sas.com.

SAS Press books are written *by* SAS Users *for* SAS Users. Please visit sas.com/books to sign up to request information on how to become a SAS Press author.

We welcome your participation in the development of new books and your feedback on SAS Press books that you are using. Please visit sas.com/books to sign up to review a book

Learn about new books and exclusive discounts. Sign up for our new books mailing list today at https://support.sas.com/en/books/subscribe-books.html.

Foreword

Analytics applies statistical methods to historical data to gain insights into potential trends. The objective is to understand those insights and apply that new knowledge effectively to improve business processes, interactions between things, relationships with customers, and many other aspects of our daily lives. However, number crunching and spreadsheets are often not as compelling as we would like them to be. Representing analytical results visually allows us to quickly and effectively convey powerful messages more persuasively. Having a tool in hand that is expressly designed to build accurate and beautiful visuals as well as publish the results to the appropriate audience is absolutely vital today.

SAS® Visual Analytics software was built to provide a dynamic range of intuitive visualization capabilities on top of very large data structures with results generated at the speed of light. Use SAS Visual Analytics as a single, powerful in-memory environment to perform visual discovery of new information and produce reports interactively to see results quickly. The software's self-service analytics capabilities are enhanced with massive scalability potential and robust governance tools. SAS Visual Analytics offers capabilities for your enterprise that can scale in terms of features, volume, and users as your business grows.

Several useful papers have been written to demonstrate how to use these techniques. We have carefully selected a handful of these from recent Global Forum contributions to introduce you to the topic and let you sample what each has to offer:

A Quick Tour of SAS® Visual Analytics 8.3: More Visual, More Analytics, by Rajiv Ramarajan and Jordan Riley Benson

SAS® Visual Analytics 8.3 introduces exciting new features to make it easier to craft beautiful reports. The new release improves efficiency by enabling report authors to reuse work done for data preparation, maintain report states across sessions, and use fewer clicks to get to a report. Users can create more compelling reports by using guides to layout the report, visual tables with graphical representations in table cells, and enhanced geo-analytics to explore geographic data. The report playback feature is a new way to present the report. Integration with the new SAS® Drive makes it easy to manage reports and share access with collaborators.

Add the "Where" to the "What" with Location Analytics in SAS® Visual Analytics 8.3, by Robby Powell

Seeing is believing: understand your data by seeing where it lives. Adding geographic context to your categorical and quantitative data through geographic visualizations can present patterns that can help you understand why things happen and what you can do to encourage that behavior or change outcomes. In this paper, you learn the geographic capabilities in SAS® Visual Analytics 8.3, how to use them, and the value they deliver.

Follow My Lead: Designing Accessible Reports by Example Using SAS® Visual Analytics, by Jesse Sookne

Your Legal, IT, or Communications department said that your reports must be accessible to people with disabilities. They might have used terms like Section 508 or WCAG. Now what? This paper leads you down the path to creating accessible reports by using SAS® Visual Analytics. It includes examples of what to do and what not to do to make your reports accessible. It provides information about which types of objects to use and how to use them in order to maximize the accessibility of your reports. You can use the information in this paper to create accessible reports, comply with your organization's accessibility requirements, and enable people with disabilities to benefit from the information that you publish.

Mastering Parameters in SAS® Visual Analytics, by Stu Sztukowski

Parameters are a set of dynamic variables in SAS® Visual Analytics that can enable developers to store a selected value of prompts, buttons, sliders, and other end-user inputs into a variable or group of variables. Often underused, parameters can give developers a powerful level of control over their reports. For example, a parameter can be used to create a dynamic X or Y axis, to dynamically combine or split variables in group roles, and to increase filtering possibilities. This paper clarifies what parameters are and how to use them and gives examples of ways that parameters can be used to enhance the end user's dashboard experience. The following examples are included: creating dynamic variable roles; creating buttons to dynamically combine and split columns; and using parameters in advanced filters across multiple data sources.

Open Visualization with SAS® Viya® and Python by Joe Indelicato

As SAS® continues to push boundaries with its cloud-based analytics ecosystem, SAS® Viya®, SAS also continues to break new ground as well! With a new initiative to become more open to developers via a robust API, and current integration with the Python package known as SWAT (Scripting Wrapper for Analytics Transfer), there are opportunities to take your in-house data science initiatives to a higher level. This paper looks at incorporating open-source graphing techniques, specifically Python's matplotlib integrated with the popular D3 visualization framework, to generate interactive plots that can spur discovery of the story your data is trying to tell you. We work through some traditional statistical programming examples via calls in Jupyter Notebook to SAS Viya. Within Jupyter, we convert our static graphs into dynamic graphs using mpld3, an open-source Python library that marries D3 to Python. Finally, we demonstrate moving our sample code into a Python microservice.

Leverage Custom Geographical Polygons in SAS® Visual Analytics, Falko Schulz

Discover how you can explore geographical maps using your own custom map regions. SAS® Visual Analytics supports several predefined geo codes including various country and sub-division lookups. However often you have your own custom polygons or shape files drawing exact boundaries of the regional overlay you are trying to explore. From generic sales regions, floor plans, or even pipe lines – there are many use cases for custom polygons in visual data analysis. Using custom regions is now easier than ever with a user-interface driven support for importing and registering these custom providers. This paper demonstrates not only the different types of custom providers supported but also shows how to leverage custom polygons within SAS® Visual Analytics by showcasing various industry examples.

A Practical Guide to Responsive Reactive Design Using SAS® Visual Analytics, by Elliot Inman, Olivia Wright, and Mark Malek

While it may seem as if you need to be an artist to create the kinds of beautiful, interesting, interactive visualizations you see on many commercial websites, you don't. All you need is a basic understanding of how HTML5 works and how human beings process visual information. In this paper, we provide guidelines for using SAS® Visual Analytics to create websites that are responsive and reactive. Responsive design relies on HTML5 technologies to dynamically adjust HTML content to the screen size and orientation of a web-connected device. This enables websites to work well on many different devices, but it can cause problems. We present guidelines that reduce trial-and-error testing and describe common responsive design issues (resized legends, squished graphs, and more). We show how to easily test the responsiveness of a report using web developer views built into Google Chrome and Mozilla Firefox, and we provide warnings for some known issues with different browsers. Reactive design focuses on how a website responds to users' interactions, in particular, the speed and sensibility of response to human input. We describe how to implement a reactive design creating a smooth workflow of finger swipes or mouse clicks, how to use white space and negative space to draw users' attention, how to use color in headers and graphs to associate related content, and other tips for enabling users to maintain a mental map of dynamic content, quickly accessing the information they need to know.

Using Custom, User-Defined SAS® Formats with SAS® Visual Analytics on SAS® Viya®, by Andrew Fagan

Are formats associated with your data? Formats that you created in SAS® using the FORMAT procedure? If you want to use SAS® Visual Analytics on SAS® Viya® with your data, you need to load your formats so that they can be found. In SAS®9, this meant adding the catalog that contained your formats to the format search path. On SAS Viya, there is an analogous task but the process is different. First, SAS Viya cannot read a SAS catalog, so you need to convert your catalog to a structure that SAS Viya understands. Next, you need to place the formats in a location where SAS Viya can find them. And finally, you need to tell SAS Viya to load the formats whenever a new session is started. This paper explores how you, as a user of SAS Visual Analytics on SAS Viya, can accomplish these steps and make your formats available. You can do this by using SAS® Environment Manager, SAS® Studio, or shell scripts. Each of these methods is described in detail, including sample code, and the benefits and limitations of each are presented.

We hope these selections give you a useful overview of the tools and techniques that are available for visual analytics on SAS® Viya®. Additionally, SAS offers free video tutorials on both visual analytics and SAS Viya. For more information, please visit https://video.sas.com/category/videos/sas-visual-analytics and https://video.sas.com/category/videos/sas-viya .

Rob Collum

Rob Collum is a Principal Technical Architect in the Professional Services Division at SAS. For the past twenty years, Rob has enabled the delivery of high-performance solutions that provide substantial value and meaningful impact to SAS customers around the world. He currently works alongside a team of professionals who partner with other divisions to identify, create, and standardize architectural practices for the newest SAS technologies. Rob received a Bachelor's degree in Computer Science from North Carolina State University, is a regular contributor to SAS Global Forum, and has coauthored several SAS certification exams.

A Quick Tour of SAS® Visual Analytics 8.3: More Visual, More Analytics

Rajiv Ramarajan and Jordan Riley Benson, SAS Institute Inc., Cary, NC

ABSTRACT

SAS® Visual Analytics 8.3 introduces exciting new features to make it easier to craft beautiful reports. The new release improves efficiency by enabling report authors to reuse work done for data preparation, maintain report states across sessions, and use fewer clicks to get to a report. Users can create more compelling reports by using guides to lay out the report, visual tables with graphical representations in table cells, and enhanced geo-analytics to explore geographic data. The report playback feature is a new way to present the report. Integration with the new SAS® Drive makes it easy to manage reports and share access with collaborators.

INTRODUCTION

SAS Visual Analytics 8.3 is designed for non-expert business users, data scientists, and tech-savvy report consumers. It provides a powerful user interface to extract insights from data and tell a story. It does this by making the building blocks of reporting more effective and easier to reuse and have more features for data manipulation and analytics. This paper provides an overview of the major enhancements in user experience for the software released in 2018.

MORE VISUAL

New additions to drag-and-drop, pop-up menu items, automatic features, and object manipulation make the user interface more visual and easier to manipulate with simple point and click actions.

INTERACTIVE USER EXPERIENCE

A precision grid in the report helps to lay out objects in the report. Resizing and moving objects is easier as positions automatically align to the grid. See Figure 1. Precision Grid. A denser grid is displayed when the Ctrl key is pressed.

Figure 1. Precision Grid

Reference lines in charts can be repositioned with a click and drag. A richer pop-up menu shown in Figure 2. Pop-up Menu enables sort, replace, or remove actions on a data item, moving an object to another page, or changing aggregation type in the data pane.

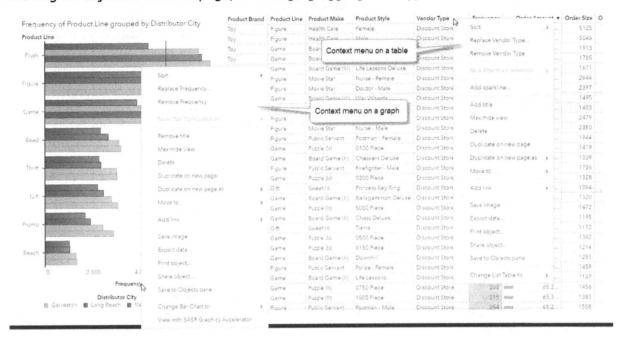

Figure 2. Pop-up Menu

Report Playback in SAS Report Viewer automatically presents the contents of a report in sequence. This is primarily used for audiences who don't navigate through the report but consume it in a more passive manner, such as at a kiosk. Settings allow the content to be displayed by page or object, show navigation, and specify the speed of the playback. See Figure 3.

Figure 3. Edit Report Playback

A report summary for a report can be embedded with live data values using point and click actions. See Figure 4. This summary can be consumed within the report, when previewing the report in SAS Drive, in report distribution emails, and in SAS Visual Analytics Apps.

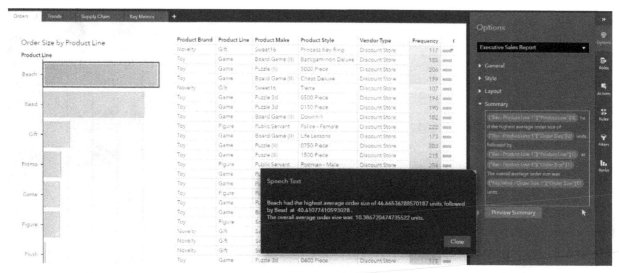

Figure 4. Report Summary

OBJECTS

Crosstabs now fit their columns to width. List tables and crosstabs have condensed row heights, which can be expanded with a setting in the options pane. List tables visualize data better with bars or a heat map within a measure column. See Figure 5.

Product Brand	Product Line	Product Make	Product Style	Vendor Type	Frequency	Order Amount ▼	Order Size	Order Sales Cost
Toy	Figure	Health Care	Female	Discount Store	745	222.9...	5125	27,160.71
Toy	Figure	Health Care	Male	Discount Store	790	188.3...	5046	26,773.76
Toy	Figure	Health Care	Female	Other	467	132.8...	3319	16,835.76
Toy	Game	Board Game (III)	Kitchen Masters	Discount Store	273	124.8...	1913	18,897.33
Toy	Figure	Health Care	Male	Other	459	123.3...	2995	15,274.03
Toy	Game	Board Game (III)	Cars	Discount Store	256	115.0...	1785	19,859.83
Toy	Game	Board Game (III)	Life Lessons Deluxe	Discount Store	279	114.5...	1671	17,239.09
Toy	Figure	Movie Star	Nurse - Female	Discount Store	385	105.7...	2644	13,316.46
Toy	Figure	Movie Star	Doctor - Male	Discount Store	352	102.8...	2397	12,695.74
Toy	Game	Board Game (III)	War Wizards	Discount Store	259	102.7...	1495	16,198.89
Toy	Game	Board Game (III)	Life Lessons Deluxe	Other	192	100.0...	1452	15,133.07
Novelty	Gift	Sweet16	Princess Magnet	Other	141	96.11...	1518	9,893.54
Toy	Game	Board Game (III)	Rise-and-Fall	Discount Store	234	95.04...	1403	13,255.38
Novelty	Gift	Sweet16	Tierra	Other	142	93.94...	1553	10,852.48
Toy	Figure	Movie Star	Doctor - Female	Discount Store	397	90.94...	2479	12,437.40
Toy	Figure	Movie Star	Nurse - Male	Discount Store	382	90.17...	2350	12,749.65

Figure 5. Cell Graphs

Bar charts can alter the spacing between the bars, which changes the bar widths. The legends in graphs in general have improved so that even when the legend is collapsed, the information is presented via a pop over. Images can be shown in the nodes of network analysis using display rules.

Navigation in a stacked container has various visual options and positions. As Figure 6 shows, stacked containers allow the use of buttons, dots, links, tabs and numbers for navigation, and they can be positioned in various alignments at the top, bottom, or sides of the container.

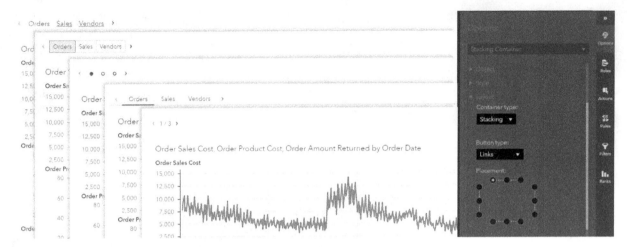

Figure 6. Navigation Options in a Stacked Container

Automatic object names and hierarchy names make it easier to track report content while building the report. This feature is especially useful during data exploration since it eliminates the need for manual name updates.

Automatic number compaction has been added to the list table, cross tab, and pie chart. See Figure 7.

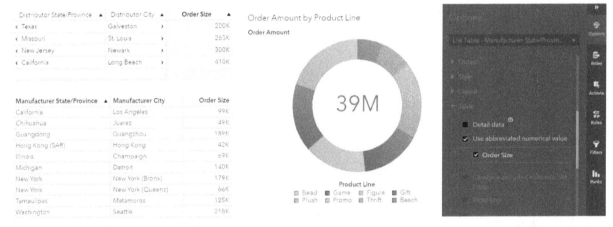

Figure 7. Number Compaction

While the user interface has become more visual, the report authoring experience has become more accessible to users with visual impairments. Keyboard navigation has been improved. Bar charts, line charts, pie charts, scatter plots, bubble plots, and time series plots can now access the SAS Graphics Accelerator, a browser plug-in that enables users with visual impairments to explore and share these graphs.

MORE REUSE

Three new features enable the reuse of data source edits, filter definitions, and object properties: Data views, common filters, and object templates. They are embedded in the existing user experience to keep it familiar but make it more efficient.

REPORT DATA VIEWS

Data views save the settings of a data source in the report. These include the filters applied, the names, formats, show/hide statuses, classifications and aggregations of the data items, any hierarchies, custom categories, and calculated items. Data views are specific to a data source. See Figure 8. A data source can have a default data view set by an administrator, and a default data view per user set by the user. Like data sources, a data view can be used across multiple reports. Modifying a data view does not affect the report.

Figure 8. Report Data Views

COMMON FILTERS

Common filters are defined once and can then be applied across multiple objects in a report. Edits to the filter affect all the objects that it is applied to. Common filters are listed in the data pane. See Figure 9.

Figure 9. Common Filters

OBJECT TEMPLATES

Object templates save the properties assigned to the object. They help to save customizations made to the properties of report objects. Saved object templates are listed in the Objects pane and can be added to the report canvas like any other objects. They do not save the data settings. See Figure 10.

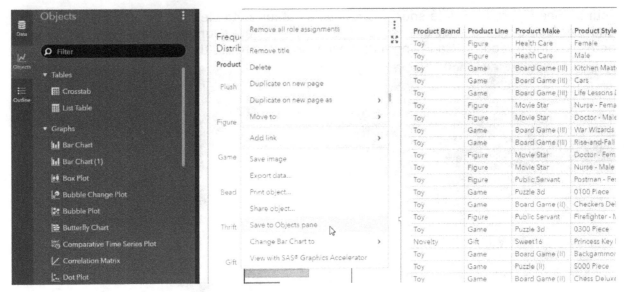

Figure 10. Object Templates

MORE DATA

An Excel spreadsheet is quickly imported into the report canvas with a simple drag-and-drop operation. Handling data is easier with the ability to join data sources and create an aggregated data source within the user interface. The one-click automated analysis object and new features in geo maps add more powerful analytics to the straightforward user experience.

DATA SOURCE JOIN

Two data sources can now be combined to create a new data source made up of data from the original data sources. The default join type is Left join, which can be changed to Right, Inner or Full joins. When two data sources are specified, the data source join is automatically based on the first column between the two data sources that have the same name. Additional conditions can be added to more accurately define the join, and output columns can be specified to limit the size of the combined data set. See Figure 11.

Figure 11. Data Source Join

AGGREGATED DATA SOURCE

A data source can be reduced by creating an aggregated data source with fewer rows and columns. The rows are aggregated based on the category variables selected and the filters assigned when creating the aggregated data source. The aggregation type of columns is based on the type in the original data source. Aggregated data sources are report-specific and generated when the report is opened. You can join two aggregated data sources if they don't have a data source filter assigned. See Figure 12.

Figure 12. Aggregated Data Source

In addition to the above, period calculations now support week, quarter, and day levels. Date-time formats now support events with millisecond precision. The new AggregateTable operator allows you to calculate aggregations of measures across values of categories that are not assigned to the object.

MORE ANALYTICS

AUTOMATED ANALYSIS

A new report object, Automated Analysis, identifies and displays the most important underlying factors for a selected response variable in a single click. See Figure 13. For measures, the object displays the four groups that show the greatest values of the measure, and two groups that show the least. For category response variable, the object shows the top four groups that contain the greatest percentage of a selected category value, and two groups that contain the least. The target category value can be changed.

The underlying factors are displayed sorted by their relative importance. Selecting an underlying factor variable highlights it in the result groups that explain the response. A visualization and explanation showing the relationship between the response variable and the selected underlying factor is also displayed.

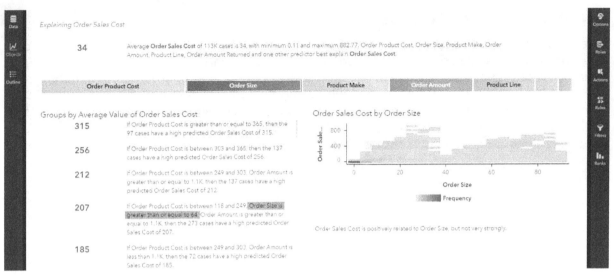

Figure 13. Automated Analysis

GEO ANALYTICS

Pins in Geo maps enable you to mark a location on the map, draw routes between two points, and select geographic areas around that location. See Figure 14. The new contour map type makes it easier to visualize dense data. Another way to visualize data is by animating the geo map across the values of a measure.

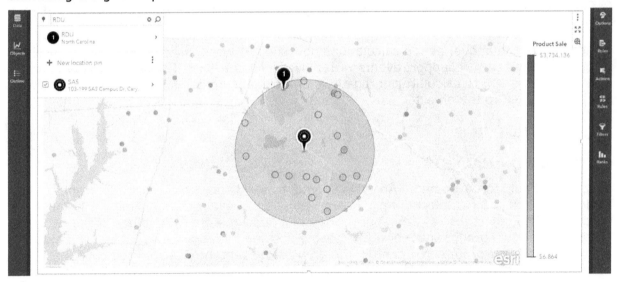

Figure 14. Pins in Geo maps

In addition to these features, the new Bayesian Network object enables visualizing effective predictive models during supervised data mining.

CONCLUSION

SAS® Visual Analytics 8.3 makes the building blocks of reporting more visual, easier to reuse, and with more features for richer data manipulation and analytics. The new features build on the strong design groundwork laid by previous releases presented analytics in an easy-to-consume user experience. The features suggest a new direction toward more flexible data handling, bringing analytics to the forefront and presenting insights – akin to storytelling.

REFERENCES

SAS Institute Inc. 2019. SAS Institute fact sheet. "SAS Visual Analytics on SAS Viya." https://www.sas.com/content/dam/SAS/en_us/doc/factsheet/sas-visual-analytics-on-sas-viya-108779.pdf, Accessed on February 24, 2019.

SAS Institute Inc. 2019. "SAS Graphics Accelerator." Accessed on February 24, 2019. http://support.sas.com/software/products/graphics-accelerator/index.html

SAS Institute Inc. 2019. "What's new in SAS Visual Analytics." Accessed on February 24, 2019. https://www.sas.com/en_us/software/visual-analytics/new-features.html

SAS Institute Inc. 2019. SAS® Visual Analytics 8.3 Documentation. Accessed on February 24, 2019. http://support.sas.com/documentation/onlinedoc/va/index.html#viya83

ACKNOWLEDGMENTS

This paper captures the work of the SAS Visual Analytics product team (product management, development, design, testing, publications, technical support, education, marketing, and field support). The team received valuable feedback from customers who engaged with us during the design and development phase. We are grateful for all their support.

RECOMMENDED READING

"Overview of SAS Visual Analytics." Video. SAS Institute Inc. Available http://video.sas.com/#category/videos/sas-visual-analytics. Accessed on March 17, 2019.

Murphy, Travis. 2016. "Infographics Powered by SAS® Visual Analytics and SAS® Office Analytics." Proceedings of the SAS Global Forum 2016 Conference. Cary, NC: SAS Institute Inc. Available https://support.sas.com/resources/papers/proceedings16/SAS3360-2016.pdf

CONTACT INFORMATION

Your comments and questions are valued and encouraged. Contact the author at:

Rajiv Ramarajan
SAS Institute Inc.
Rajiv.Ramarajan@sas.com
www.sas.com

Jordan Riley Benson
SAS Institute Inc.
Riley.Benson@sas.com
www.sas.com

Add the "Where" to the "What" with Location Analytics in SAS® Visual Analytics 8.3

Robby Powell, SAS

ABSTRACT

Seeing is believing—understand your data by seeing where it lives. Adding geographic context to your categorical and quantitative data through location analytics can present patterns to help you understand why things happen and what you can do to encourage that behavior or change outcomes. In this paper, you learn the geographic capabilities of SAS® Visual Analytics 8.3 Location Analytics, how to use them, and the value they deliver.

INTRODUCTION

Most of the data we generate and consume includes location information. Mailing address is clearly location. Sales Territories are regions which are also location, and of course GPS latitude/longitude is location. Including location in your visualizations adds a new perspective of "where" to your business analysis.

Every**THING** we interact with, monitor, or measure has a location: buildings, vehicles, people, roads, power and water lines, mountains, rivers, and so on.

Some of these things are stationary and others change position regularly, but they all have location. Visualizing how the location of these **THINGS** in your world interact and influence your business goals can offer tremendous insight.

In this paper you will learn about the Location Analytics capabilities in SAS Visual Analytics 8.3 and how to use them. By addressing multiple use cases using SAS Visual Analytics you will understand how to leverage the native location capabilities and deep integration with Esri to add the "where" to the "what" in your data visualizations.

SAS Visual Analytics Location Analytics capabilities include:

- **Displaying your data on a map**.

- **Custom Regions** – Define bounded areas such as states, counties, sales territories, and even stadium seats. Custom shapefiles can be added to SAS Visual Analytics as regions. These regions can be colored based on measures or categories in your data.

- **Points of Interest** – Set a point on a map or "drop a pin" and explore that location and the area around that location. Including geographic selection, demographics and geo-search.

- **Routing** – How to get from one point of interest to another in an optimal fashion.

- **Viewing Dense Data on a Map** (Clustering and Contours) - If you have dense data, proximity clustering and contour maps provide ways to visualize data and identify location clusters and patterns.

- **Map Layers** - Add map overlays to your maps to provide deeper context to the "where" in your data on a map. For instance, if the data being displayed is store locations, adding a highway layer and a railroads layer will help you understand the proximity of store locations to transportation corridors.

- **Geocoding** – Augment your data by adding latitude and longitude values for each record based on the location data you already have. That way, you can easily add your data to a map.

The use cases being addressed in this paper apply to a Business Analyst being asked to explore the following:

1. forest fire data to propose locations for Fire Shelters for future fire disasters,

2. forest fire impact at the county level to search for ways counties can be convinced to combine efforts earlier and proactively,

3. forest fire outbreaks to determine policy, outreach, and educational efforts that can be applied to reduce the number of future forest fires.

DISPLAYING YOUR DATA ON A MAP

To display your data in a Geo Map object in SAS Visual Analytics you start by creating a **Geographic Item** from the **+ New data item** in the Data Pane, as shown in Figure 1.

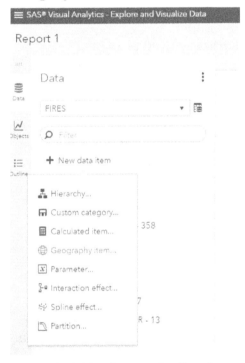

Figure 1. Add a Geography item to your data.

You can then specify the name of the **Geographic Item**, the category or measure to base the **Geographic Item**, and the **Geography data type** as shown in Figure 2.

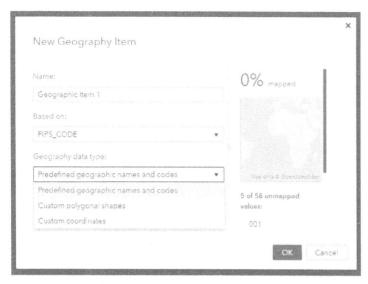

Figure 2. New Geography Item.

Based on the data being presented and the types of explorations being supported, you will determine whether to present the geographic data as coordinate data points, or as regions. Regardless, displaying data on a map requires location information to be present.

To display your data as coordinate data points you must have latitude and longitude information in your data. If latitude and longitude do not exist and you have other location data, you can Geocode your data to add latitude and longitude columns through the **Manage Data** action in SAS Visual Analytics, as shown in Figure 3. The geocoding operations calls the Esri geocode service to return latitude and longitude values. Note to access this capability, you must have an account with Esri and enter your Esri credentials in your SAS Visual Analytics settings.

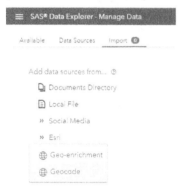

Figure 3. Geocode your data to add latitude and longitude columns.

Select the **Geography data type**: **Custom coordinates** and enter the **latitude and longitude** measures (columns), as shown in Figure 4.

Figure 4. New Geography Item - Custom coordinates.

The location data is evaluated, and the correctness of your mapping is determined – 100%, not bad. This feedback lets you understand the quality of your geographic data, so you can consider resolving data quality issues and possibly receive better results. Now drag **Geographic Item 1** to the report palette, SAS Visual Analytics recognizes the **Geographic Item** dragged to the report and renders the points on a **GeoMap object** as shown in Figure 5. Now edit the options, roles, actions, and other settings to set the data, presentation, and interactions to meet your exact requirements and expectations.

Figure 5. Data points on a GeoMap.

CUSTOM REGIONS

Regions shown on a map clearly display bounded areas such as countries, states, sales territories, and more as shown in the California Counties map in Figure 6. This report uses color saturation to represent the number of fire days for each county. Interactively filtering between the map and table of named fires shows the opportunities for cross-county collaboration.

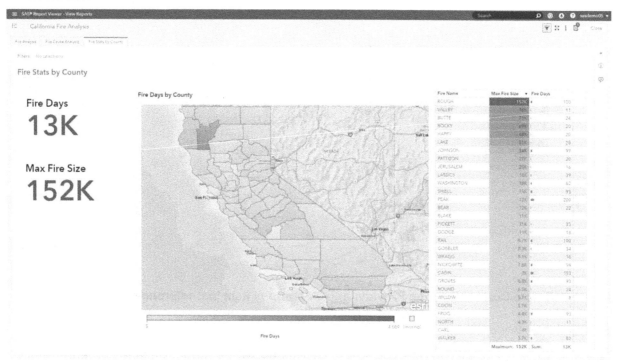

Figure 6. Fire Statistics for California counties.

With a little more effort and the use of a GIS tool, non-geographic maps can be created to display regions such as rooms in a conference hall or seats in a stadium. This paper does not cover this topic. Please refer to the paper from the SAS Global 2018 Conference, "Leverage custom geographical polygons in SAS® Visual Analytics."

Out of the box, SAS Visual Analytics provides built-in regions for countries and US states that you can use in your reports. To add custom regions to your reports you need to import a GIS Shapefile into SAS Visual Analytics and create a **Custom Polygon Provider**.

The SAS Macro, %shpimprt, is one way to import GIS Shapefiles into SAS Visual Analytics for use as the source for a custom polygon provider. See SAS Viya Documentation for information on how to do this. Figure 6 uses the California counties shapefile from the California Open Data Portal (data.ca.gov). The %shpimport SAS Macro was used to convert and load the shapefile data.

The next step is to create a **Custom Polygon Provider**. To do this, your data to be visualized as regions on a map must share a common value (shared index) with the custom polygon provider (shape file) to serve as the join variable for the two data sources. The California counties value COUNTYFP and the FIRES value FIPS_CODE are common and will be used to join the tables, as seen in Figure 7. This Custom polygon provider is created with **ID Column**: COUNTYFP and the is created with the **Geography Item Region ID**: FIPS_CODE, see Figure 7.

5

Figure 7. Create Custom Polygon Provider and Geography Item that references it.

POINTS OF INTEREST

"Drop a Pin" – it's what you often do when interacting with a map. You want to learn about a point of interest, so you drop a pin and investigate. SAS Visual Analytics supports Points of Interest allowing you to:

- Drop a Pin
- Geographic Selection
- Demographics
- Geo-search

DROP A PIN

Designate points of interest by dropping pins on a map as shown in Figure 8.

6

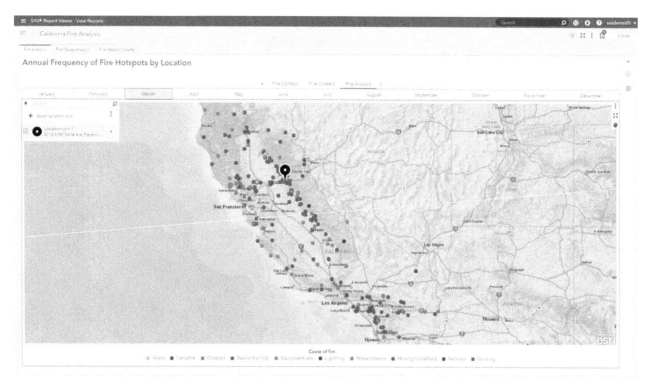

Figure 8. Drop a pin and learn more about a location.

For instance, if you were asked to identify areas to build fire shelters, you would look for areas of high fire activity in past years. After dropping a pin, your exploration begins.

GEOGRAPHIC SELECTION

Understanding proximity of a proposed shelter to past fires can aid your decision. To visualize this, make geographic selections based on distance, travel-distance, or travel-time. Using the **Travel-distance Geographic Selection** selects all fires within the travel distances specified. For example, 5- and 10-mile drive distances selections as shown in Figure 9Figure 10.

Figure 9. Make a geographic selection.

Based on the large number of fires captured in the geographic selection area in Figure 10 it makes sense to continue evaluating this location as a possible fire shelter site. Distance geographic selection is included out of the box with SAS Visual Analytics. Geographic selections for Travel distance and Travel time require access to your Esri account.

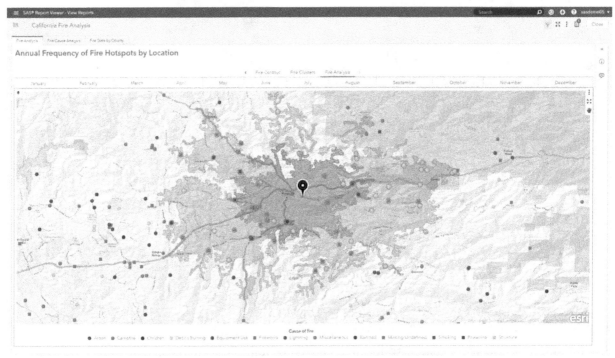

Figure 10. 5- and 10-mile Geographic Selections from the specified pin.

DEMOGRAPHICS

Fire shelters are intended to serve the community in times of need, so it is important to understand the population being served. Leveraging the SAS Visual Analytics integration with Esri, demographic information can be chosen and shown directly on the map during exploration as shown in Figure 11 and Figure 12. Demographics information requires access to your Esri account.

Figure 11. Select Demographics information for the Geographic Selection area.

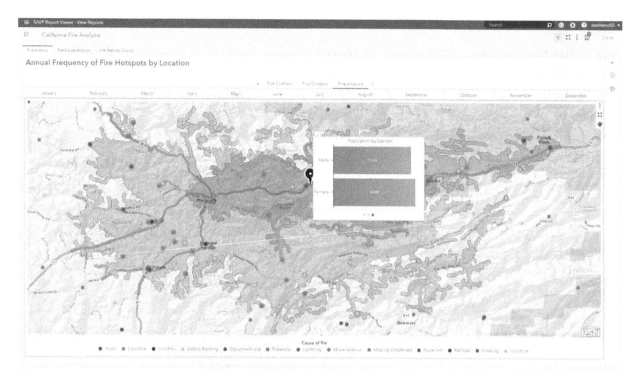

Figure 12. Population by Gender for the Geographic Selection.

From the demographics information we can tell that the male and female population for the area is very similar. This information will aid in stocking supplies for this shelter.

GEO-SEARCH

It is also important for fire shelters to be located near locations such as hospitals for fire shelter visitors in need of medical, and grocery stores to restock supplies. Figure 13 shows a geo-search of nearby grocery stores.

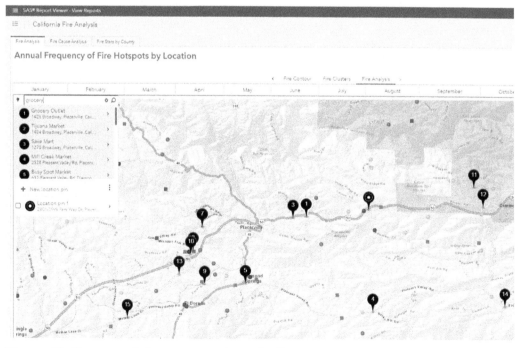

Figure 13. Geo-search for grocery stores in the area.

ROUTING

How is the best way to get from here to there? We now know that there are grocery stores nearby, but what is the best route to get there?

Taking the geo-search results, we select search pin #1 "Grocery Outlet" and route from that point back to the proposed shelter location as seen in Figure 14.

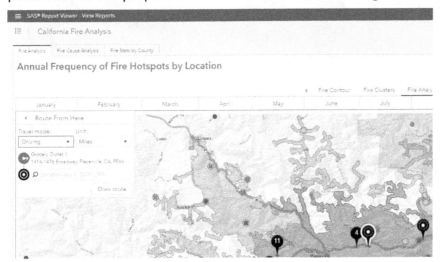

Figure 14. Drawing routes between pins.

Various travel modes: Direct, Driving, Trucking, Walking can be used to draw routes as shown in Figure 15 and Figure 16. Routing uses the Esri routing service called through your Esri account.

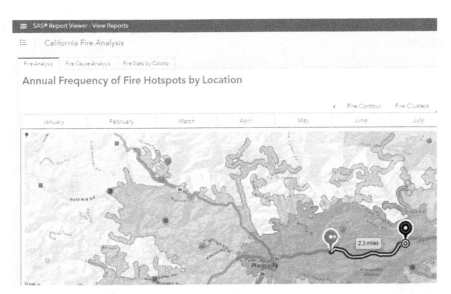

Figure 15. Driving route between points.

Figure 16. Routes from grocery store and hospital to the proposed fire shelter.

VIEWING DENSE DATA ON A MAP

Relying on a single view of your data may lead to an incorrect assessment. To get the complete picture, it is important to view various perspectives before acting. An example of this involves displaying dense data points on geographic maps. In situations where there is high saturation of data there is risk of coincident data points which overlap and hide other data points. SAS Visual Analytics provides options for gaining insight into dense data.

The illusion caused by dense data can mask the intensity in highly saturated areas as shown in Figure 17.

Figure 17. Dense data displayed on a map.

In this map you can see that there were many fire hotspots in California. You can see where the fires occurred and where fires did not but speculating beyond that is risky.

PROXIMITY CLUSTERING

One way to provide clarity in this situation is Proximity Clustering as shown in Figure 18.

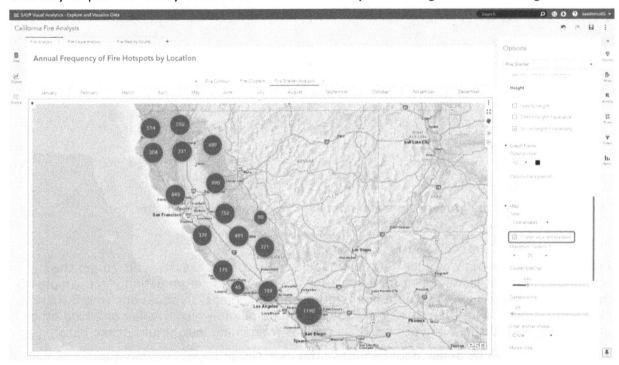

Figure 18. Gain insight from dense data with Proximity Clustering.

If you are displaying Coordinate points on a map (points displayed based on latitude, longitude), then the **Cluster adjacent markers** option is available. Simply select that option and your data is clustered, allowing you to see the areas of high saturation and how areas relate to one another based on the frequency number displayed as part of each cluster bubble. In this mode, as you zoom in and zoom out the clusters are recalculated. Zooming in eventually results in singleton data points being displayed as there is enough sparsity for the clusters to no longer be useful.

CONTOUR MAPS

Another way to provide clarity when dealing with dense data on a map is by using **Contour Map** which is shown in Figure 19.

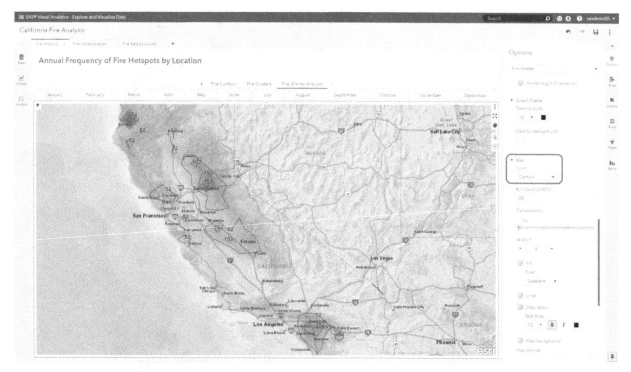

Figure 19. Gain insight from dense data with Contour Maps.

Simply change the **Map Type** to **Contour** and the map is displayed with color saturation based on the **Color Data Role**. You can specify the precision of your contour map by setting options including:

1. Bin count: specifies the number of grids to use when clustering. The higher the number of bins, the closer together the contour lines will be and the smaller and more precise the contours are drawn.

2. Levels: the maximum number of contour levels to display.

3. Lines: displays an outline around each contour level on the map.

WEB MAPS AND MAP LAYERS

"An ArcGIS web map is an interactive display of geographic information that you can use to tell stories and answer questions.", "Esri ArcGIS Online – Web maps", doc.arcgis.com/en/arcgis-online/reference/what-is-web-map.htm. You can create custom web maps in Esri ArcGIS Online to provide geographical information using publicly available geographic data or private data that only you can access. Figure 20 is a web map displaying map layers for railroads, hydrocarbon pipelines, and parks. This web map was created with publicly available geographic data and will be used to help answer questions about wildfire data.

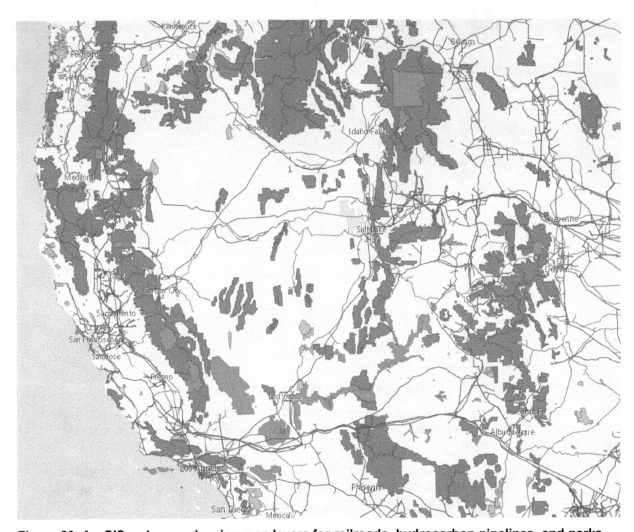

Figure 20. ArcGIS web map showing map layers for railroads, hydrocarbon pipelines, and parks.

To include web maps in SAS Visual Analytics, you just add a Data-Driven Content object to your report. See SAS Documentation for information about working with the Data-Driven Content object.

You will need to build and host the sas-visual-analytics-geowebmap project from the SAS GitHub site, and include the URL for the web app as the *URL property* in your Data-Driven Content object. Modify your URL using the Query string arguments shown in Figure 21.

Query string arguments

Argument	Description
visualizationType	Optional. Possible values include "scatter", "bubble", or "choropleth". If unspecified, the value will be inferred from other arguments or left as "scatter".
x	The label of the column containing longitude expressed in the same terms as the base map. Defaults to "Longitude". Required for scatter and bubble visualizations.
y	The label of the column containing latitude expressed in the same terms as the base map. Defaults to "Latitude". Required for scatter and bubble visualizations.
size	The label of the column containing the size measurement. Required for bubble visualizations.
color	The label of the column containing the color measurement. Optional for bubble and choropleth visualizations.
animation	The label of the column containing the date used when animating through the data. Optional. Animations are not currently supported in choropleths or 3D views, and they should be considered experimental. It has been observed that performance degrades rapidly when the data's row count enters the tens of thousands. Acceptable date formats are those correctly interpreted by Moment, which include RFC2822 and ISO formats.
colorMin	A hex, rgba, or named color for the minimum value of the range. Defaults to "#bfe4e7" (also expressed, for example, as "rgba(191,228,231,1)", which is somewhat close to "LightCyan").
colorMax	A hex, rgba, or named color for the minimum value of the range. Defaults to "#00929f". Also controls dot color for the scatter plot as well as default color for the choropleth (when no color column is assigned).
outline	A hex, rgba, or named color for an outline on drawn shapes. Defaults to "#007E88". Also controls highlight color for 3D views.
geoId	The label of the column containing the geographic identifiers for the areas to be drawn. Required for choropleth.
featureServiceUrl	The url to the Esri feature service containing the shapes of the geographies identified by the geoId. Required for choropleth.
featureServiceGeoId	The name of the attribute in the Esri feature service that will match values found in the geoId column of the VA data. Required for choropleth.
featureServiceWhere	A where clause to be provided to the Esri feature service that filters results. Optional.
featureServiceMaxAllowableOffset	The optional maxAllowableOffset provided to the feature service. Can be used to restrict the amount of detail (and thus transmission size) of the geographic shapes it returns.
portalItemId	The ID for a web map served at arcgis.com. Optional. Defaults to basemap "osm" (OpenStreetMap).
baseMap	The ID for a basemap from arcgis.com (e.g., "streets", "satellite", "hybrid"). Optional. Defaults to basemap "osm" (OpenStreetMap). Ignored if portalItemId is set.
use3D	Set to "true" to display the map in a 3D SceneView. Defaults to false.
title	The title of the layer that includes VA data. Optional. Defaults to the geoId, if available, or to "SAS VA Layer", if not.
zIndex	The index of the layer that includes VA data. Optional. Use "0" to insert the layer below all others. Defaults to the top-most level.
featuresMax	The maximum number of features allowed in the SAS layer. Optional. If set, the user will receive a warning when the data's row count exceeds this number, and the SAS layer will be cleared.
period	Defines the interval used to subdivide the animation date. Valid values are units of time accepted by Moment (e.g., "millisecond", "day", "month", "year"). Defaults to "year".
useSmartLegends	Set to "true" to use Esri's "smart mapping" legends for color and size (where appropriate). Defaults to false. This feature is experimental.
useSampleData	Set to "true" to load data from SampleData.json instead of VA. Useful for testing. Optional.

Figure 21. Geowebmap project Query String Arguments, from the SAS GitHub site.

The SAS Visual Analytics report in Figure 22 shows the web map combined with SAS Visual Analytics data points. From this visualization, you can see that many of the wildfires occurring in March tend to follow the western border of park land. This insight may indicate the need to better educate landowners whose land backs up to park land on appropriate strategies to reduce forest fires.

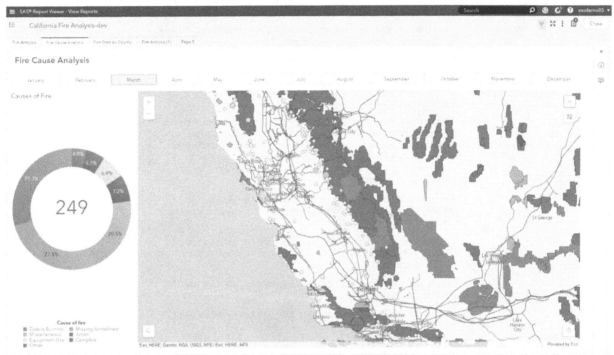

Figure 22. SAS Visual Analytics data combined with a web map, in a data-driven content object.

The standard SAS Visual Analytics data interactions, such as filtering and brushing, are supported between the web map visualization and the other objects in the report. The web map layers can also be toggled on and off through the drop-down menu on the map, as seen in Figure 23.

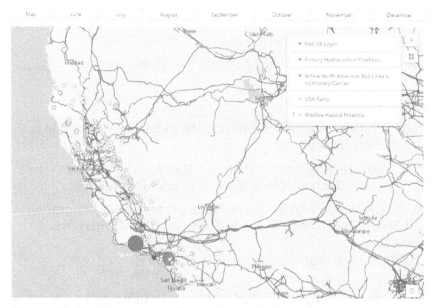

Figure 23. Toggle on and off map layers in the web map.

Using the SAS Visual Analytics Location Analytics capabilities presented in this paper, the Business Analyst is now able to present a case for:

1. Proposed fire shelter locations for next fire season, based on previous years data, proximity and routes to necessary points of interest (hospital, grocery), and demographics information about the local population.

2. Describe opportunities for counties to work together to proactively address wildfires.

3. Policy, outreach, and educational efforts to reduce the number of future forest fires by reaching out to property owners who own land adjacent to park land.

CONCLUSION

Most of the data we generate and consume includes location. SAS Visual Analytics provides a wide range of location analytics through native capabilities and integration with Esri ArcGIS Online. Adding location analytics to your reports and explorations magnifies your insight to address your use cases and support your decisions.

REFERENCES

We acknowledge the use of data and imagery from LANCE FIRMS operated by the NASA/GSFC/Earth Science Data and Information System (ESDIS) with funding provided by NASA/HQ. MODIS Collection 6 NRT Hotspot / Active Fire Detections MCD14DL. Available on-line [https://earthdata.nasa.gov/firms] DOI: 10.5067/FIRMS/MODIS/MCD14DL.NRT.006

Schulz, Falko, "Leverage custom geographical polygons in SAS® Visual Analytics," *Proceedings of the SAS Global 2018 Conference.* Cary, NC, SAS Institute Inc. Available at: https://www.sas.com/content/dam/SAS/support/en/sas-global-forum-proceedings/2018/1732-2018.pdf

SAS Institute Inc. 2019. "SAS® Viya® Administration: Data – Loading Geographic Polygon Data as a CAS Table," https://go.documentation.sas.com/?docsetId=caldatamgmtcas&docsetTarget=p1dwawsidsc zlpn121j0glleicxp.htm&docsetVersion=3.4&locale=en

RECOMMENDED READING

Report Images: *"SAS Visual Analytics Gallery."* Available at:
https://communities.sas.com/t5/SAS-Visual-Analytics-Gallery/tkb-p/vagallery

- YouTube Video: *"Location Analytics – Where things happen."* Available at:
  https://www.youtube.com/watch?v=5P_oiFf-xh4

- SAS Global Forum 2019 Conference Papers:
  - Phillips, Jeff, Hicks, Scott, and Graham, Tony "Introduction to Esri Integration in Visual Analytics," Cary, NC, SAS Institute Inc.
  - Phillips, Jeff, Hicks, Scott, and Graham, Tony, "There's a Map for That! What's new and coming soon in SAS Mapping Technologies," Cary, NC, SAS Institute Inc.

Nori, Murali and Patel, Himesh, "New Location Analysis and Demographic Data Integration with SAS® Visual Analytics and Esri," *Proceedings of the SAS Global 2018 Conference.* Cary, NC, SAS Institute Inc. Available at:
https://www.sas.com/content/dam/SAS/support/en/sas-global-forum-proceedings/2018/1801-2018.pdf

Murphy, Travis and Schulz, Falko, "Supercharge Your Dashboards with Infographic Concepts Using SAS® Visual Analytics," *Proceedings of the SAS Global 2018 Conference.* Cary, NC, SAS Institute Inc. Available at: https://www.sas.com/content/dam/SAS/support/en/sas-global-forum-proceedings/2018/2069-2018.pdf

Aanderud, Tricia, "Finding the Treasure: Using Geospatial Data for Better Results with SAS® Visual Analytics," *Proceedings of the SAS Global 2018 Conference.* Cary, NC, Zencos Consulting, Available at: https://www.sas.com/content/dam/SAS/support/en/sas-global-forum-proceedings/2018/1955-2018.pdf

CONTACT INFORMATION

Your comments and questions are valued and encouraged. Contact the author at:

Robby Powell
SAS
www.sas.com
robby.powell@sas.com
linkedin.com/in/robbypowell

Paper SAS3346-2019

Follow My Lead: Designing Accessible Reports by Example Using SAS® Visual Analytics

Jesse Sookne, SAS Institute Inc.

ABSTRACT

Your Legal, IT, or Communications department said that your reports must be accessible to people with disabilities. They might have used terms like "Section 508" or "WCAG". Now what? This paper leads you down the path to creating accessible reports by using SAS® Visual Analytics. It includes examples of what to do—and what not to do—to make your reports accessible. It provides information about which types of objects to use and how to use them in order to maximize the accessibility of your reports. You can use the information in this paper to create accessible reports, comply with your organization's accessibility requirements, and enable people with disabilities to benefit from the information that you publish.

INTRODUCTION

Many organizations, whether public or private, must comply with accessibility laws and policies. If you work in such an organization, you might have been asked whether your SAS Visual Analytics reports comply with accessibility standards. You might wonder what these standards are, and how do you comply with them?

Fortunately, you can craft your SAS Visual Analytics reports to comply with the most commonly used technical standard for digital accessibility, which is the *Web Content Accessibility Guidelines*, version 2.0. Also known as WCAG 2.0, this standard is used widely in industry, educational organizations, and governments worldwide. It has these three levels of conformance:

- Level A: basic accessibility features

- Level AA: generally accessible to people with a variety of different abilities (this is the most commonly used level)

- Level AAA: enhanced accessibility

Many national and provincial accessibility laws incorporate WCAG 2.0 AA as their technical standard. For example, both Section 508 in the United States and the Accessibility for Ontarians with Disabilities Act in Ontario, Canada, incorporate WCAG 2.0 AA. Using the information in this paper, you can design SAS Visual Analytics reports that comply with WCAG 2.0 level AA. These are the most important factors that determine compliance:

- The choices you make when authoring a report, such as which types of report objects to use

- The viewer application used to view your report

SAS Visual Analytics 8.3 comes with these four viewer applications:

- SAS Report Viewer: the HTML5 web-based viewer application

- SAS Visual Analytics App for iOS: the native iOS viewer

- SAS Visual Analytics App for Android: the native Android viewer

- SAS Visual Analytics App for Windows: the native Windows 10 viewer

As of the publication date of this paper, SAS Visual Analytics App for iOS has the highest level of accessibility. This is partly due to the iOS operating system itself having a high level of accessibility. iOS devices include an excellent built-in screen reader called VoiceOver. The VoiceOver screen reader, available on iPhones and iPads, is widely used by people who have visual impairments or blindness. SAS Visual Analytics App for iOS has powerful accessibility features, including sonification, which is the ability to present data using sound. For more information about the accessibility features of SAS Visual Analytics App for iOS, see the document *SAS Visual Analytics App 8.35 for iOS: Accessibility Features*.

This paper uses the recommendations in the document *Creating Accessible Reports Using SAS® Visual Analytics 7.4*. While those recommendations cover SAS Visual Analytics version 7.4, this paper is based on SAS Visual Analytics version 8.3.1 and SAS Visual Analytics App for iOS version 8.35. The information described in this paper also generally applies to SAS Visual Analytics 7.4 and later when used with the latest version of SAS Visual Analytics App for iOS.

To comply with WCAG 2.0 AA, follow the recommendations in the document above, along with the suggestions and examples in this paper, and inform the consumers of your reports that SAS Visual Analytics App for iOS offers the most accessible viewing experience.

PREPARATION

Much of the work of creating a report comes in the preparation. Choosing your primary message, identifying your audience, and thoroughly understanding your data are all important steps. This paper covers these topics only to the extent necessary to walk you through the process of creating an accessible report. For more detailed information about these topics, see the 2017 SAS Global Forum paper *Data Can Be Beautiful: Crafting a Compelling Story with SAS® Visual Analytics*. (See the References section of this paper.)

This paper discusses an example report about crime in the town of Cary, North Carolina, where SAS Institute is headquartered. The main objective of the report is to share facts about the town – specifically about crime in the town, though other supporting facts, like population, are included. Most of the data comes from the town itself and requires only minor cleanup. (See the References section of this paper.) The report includes ten years of data, from 2009 to 2018. The report uses these data items:

Category:

- Area: geographic area names, for example, "Walnut Plaza"
- Crime Category: general crime categories, for example, "Larceny"
- Crime Type: specific crime categories, for example, "Larceny – Shoplifting"
- Date: the date the incident began, in MMDDYYYY format, for example, "01/15/2009"
- Day of Week: the day of the week, for example, "Tuesday"
- Larceny + Burglary: a custom category that categorizes crimes as Larceny, Burglary, or Other
- Month: the calendar month, for example, "February"

Geography:

- Location: the latitude and longitude coordinates of the incident

Measure:

- Crimes: the number of police incidents

Aggregated Measure:

- Frequency Percent

The general public is the intended audience for this report. This is a large and diverse audience that includes people with disabilities.

The report tells the story of crime in the town of Cary. Its purpose is to answer several high-level questions:

- How frequently do various types of crimes occur?
- What are the long-term patterns or trends in the crime rate?
- Do certain crimes occur more often on particular days of the week?
- Where do crimes occur?

The report is broken into five sections: an introduction and one section for each of the questions above.

1. Intro: basic facts about the town (such as population, cost of living, and median income) along with a table of contents

2. Crime Types: the most prevalent types of crime along with a sidebar about larceny

3. Long-Term Trends: crimes over the 10-year period of the data, plus a repeating seasonal pattern

4. Day of Week: crimes by day of week, plus a weekly pattern

5. Geographic Area: crimes by area within the town, including locations plotted on a map

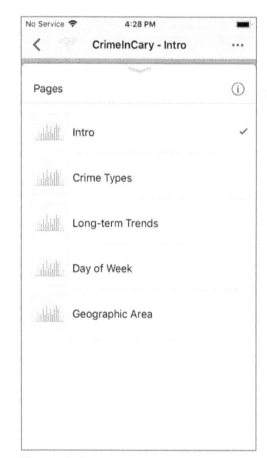

Figure 1: Pages in the Crime in Cary Example Report

OBJECTS

The set of objects you use to build your report greatly affects its accessibility. Choose objects that the paper *Creating Accessible Reports Using SAS® Visual Analytics 7.4* identifies as being accessible, and then use those objects in accessible ways as described here.

The example report uses a variety of objects:

- List Table

- Bar Chart
- Geo Map
- Line Chart
- Pie Chart
- Time Series plot
- Drop-down list
- Standard Container
- Text

The accessibility of each of these objects, with the exception of Standard Container, is described in *Creating Accessible Reports Using SAS® Visual Analytics 7.4*. Using a Standard Container generally does not affect report accessibility. In addition, the Drop-down List object is fully compliant with WCAG 2.0 AA.

TEXT

The Intro page of the example report makes heavy use of text objects – in fact, those are the only objects in the page.

Figure 2: Intro Page of the Crime in Cary Report

By default, text objects comply with WCAG 2.0 AA. Users with disabilities can generally use and understand text objects. However, it's still possible to introduce accessibility problems that can cause the object not to meet WCAG 2.0 AA. An example is selecting a background color that has insufficient contrast with foreground text. Compare the two objects in Figures 3 and 4 – one of them passes minimum contrast requirements and one does not.

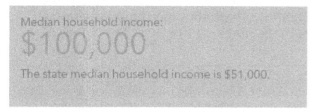

Figure 3: Text With Poor Contrast   **Figure 4: Text With Sufficient Contrast**

Use default colors to create objects that generally have sufficient contrast. Although SAS Visual Analytics App for iOS includes a theme override feature that allows users to override the colors and styles in your report with a high contrast theme, not all users will be aware of, or want to use, this option. It is best to choose colors that pass the WCAG guidelines for minimum contrast. For more information, see *Contrast (Minimum)*, WCAG Success Criterion 1.4.3.

You could also introduce formatting that conveys meaning in a way that is not accessible. Colors used in text objects cannot be perceived by users of the VoiceOver screen reader, and people with color deficient vision might not be able to perceive the colors either. However, this is generally not a problem if you follow these guidelines:

- Your use of color is decorative – that is, color is not used to convey meaning.
- You use both color and something else that is accessible to convey the same meaning.

For example, in the text object in Figure 5, color is used decoratively. You do not need the color to understand all of the information presented.

Crime index:

77

The U.S. average is 236.

Figure 5: Color Used Decoratively in a Text Object

Instead of using the decorative color in Figure 5, suppose you decided to color the Cary crime index value green if it is below the U.S. average or red if it's above the U.S. average, as shown in Figure 6.

Crime index:

77

Figure 6: Color Used to Convey Meaning in a Text Object

This use of color to convey meaning prevents people with visual impairments that affect perception of color or contrast from understanding the data in the object. It also prevents your report from complying with WCAG 2.0 AA. Because color is the only way to tell whether the Cary crime index is above or below the U.S. average, people with such visual impairments might not be able to perceive this information.

BAR CHART

The main objects in both the Crime Types and Day of Week pages of the example report are bar charts. The Crime Types page uses a horizontal bar chart showing the most common crimes by type. The Day of Week page uses a vertical bar chart showing the number of crimes by day of week.

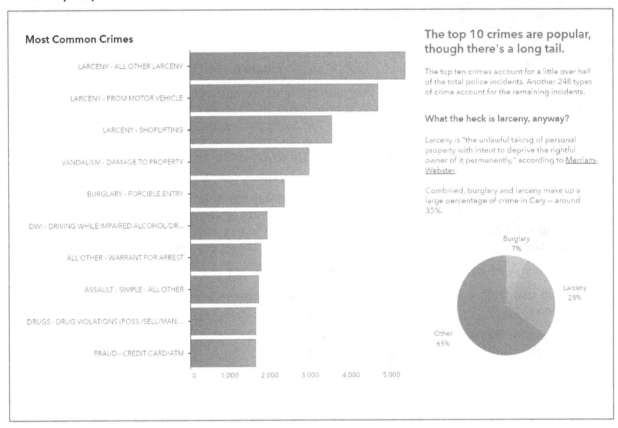

Figure 7: Crime Types Page, Bar Chart of the Most Common Crimes

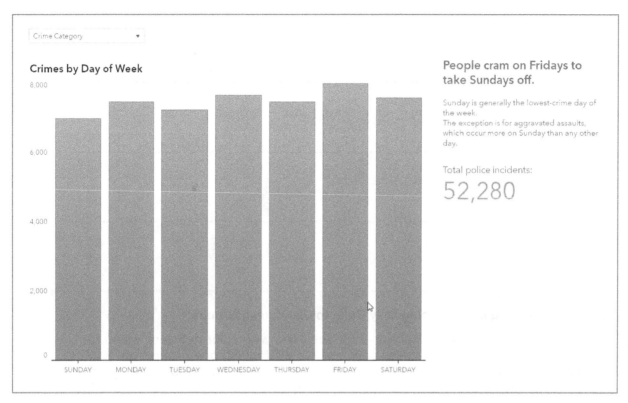

Figure 8: Day of Week Page, Bar Chart of Crimes by Day of Week

While bar charts comply with WCAG 2.0 AA by default, it's important to avoid using them in ways that cause them not to comply. Both of the bar charts in Figure 7 and 8 use a single measure and they both avoid grouping. That's good, because as of the publication date of this paper, including multiple measures or grouping in a SAS Visual Analytics bar chart prevents it from complying with WCAG 2.0 AA. Charts with these features would be non-compliant because SAS Visual Analytics distinguishes groups and measures from one another using color alone, rather than using color in addition to another feature such as a fill pattern.

One way to work around this issue is to use filtering instead of grouping. Suppose that you wanted to show the prevalence of crimes by day of week, grouped by crime category, as in Figure 9.

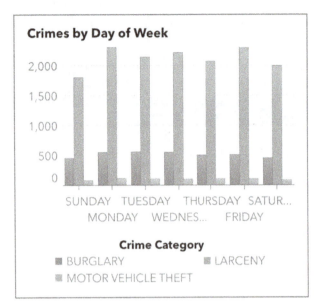

Figure 9: Grouped Bar Chart Using Only Color to Distinguish Groups

This chart can be difficult or impossible for someone with color deficient vision to understand, because the chart uses only color to distinguish one group from another. Instead, you could show a non-grouped bar chart, and let the person viewing your report choose the crime category using a filter, as in Figure 10.

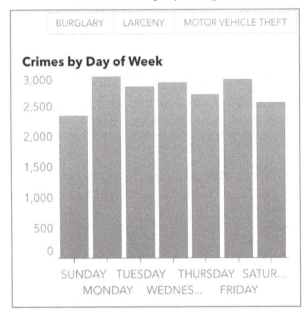

Figure 10: Bar Chart Using a Filter Instead of Grouping

While this technique might not work perfectly for all types of data, it's effective in many situations to avoid the problem of using color alone to distinguish between groups. In a future release of SAS Visual Analytics, SAS plans to introduce fill patterns for bar charts that include groups or multiple measures.

PIE CHART

Pie charts can be used in ways that comply with WCAG 2.0 AA. In general, pie charts are best used under these criteria:

- You want to emphasize the relationship between the size of a slice and the size of the whole pie.
- You have a very small number of slices (no more than three). (Gabrielle)

For example, Figure 11 illustrates appropriate data to show in a pie chart.

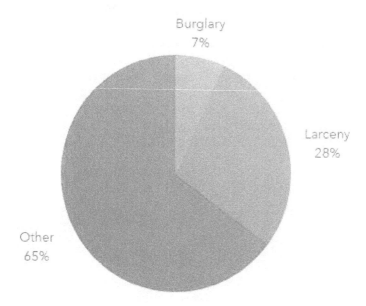

Figure 11: Pie Chart Using Color and Other Factors to Convey Meaning

While this pie chart uses color to convey meaning, it does not use color alone. To illustrate this point, try to understand the black-and-white version of the pie chart in Figure 12 (which can look quite a lot like the color version in Figure 11, if you've printed this paper on a black-and-white printer).

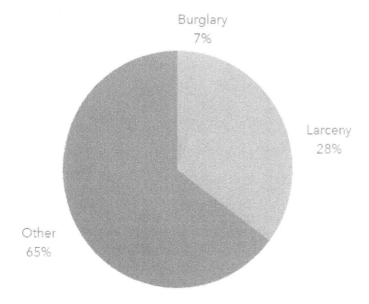

Figure 12: Pie Chart Still Understandable Without Color

You'll probably have no trouble understanding the pie chart in Figure 12, even though it's in black-and-white. In fact, you don't even need to be able to see the slices to glean the information from this pie chart, because the categories and their values are printed in the labels, which are sufficient on their own.

To make a pie chart comply with WCAG 2.0 AA, enable the **Category labels** and **Actual values** options. and set **Data label location** to **Outside**, in the pie chart object's properties.

TIME SERIES PLOT AND LINE CHART

The Long-Term Trends section of the example report uses both Time Series Plot objects and Line Chart objects. These two types of objects are very similar when it comes to accessibility, so this paper addresses them together. Both the Time Series Plot and Line Chart comply with WCAG 2.0 AA as used in the example report, and these objects are generally good choices for accessibility. However, as with most objects, it's possible to use these objects in ways that don't comply.

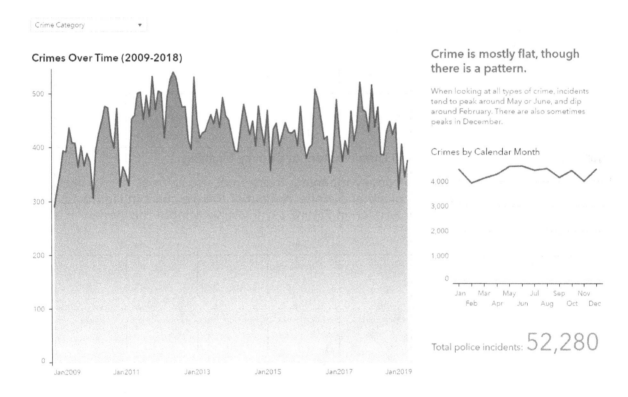

Figure 13: The Long-term Trends Page

As with bar charts, it's important to avoid using only color to convey meaning in line charts and time series plots. This matters when you are using one of these objects to display multiple measures, or when you're using grouping. Luckily, with both line charts and time series plots, there's an easy option to bring grouped charts or charts with multiple measures into compliance. Compare the three charts in Figures 14, 15, and 16.

10

Crimes by Calendar Month

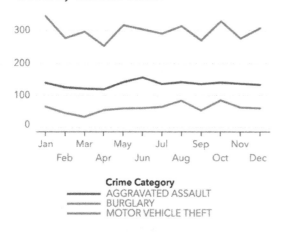

Figure 14: Chart Using Only Color to Distinguish Lines

Crimes by Calendar Month

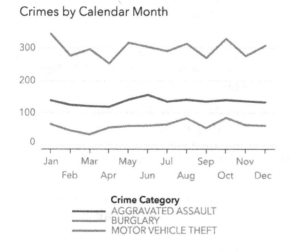

Figure 15: Chart From Figure 14, Without Color

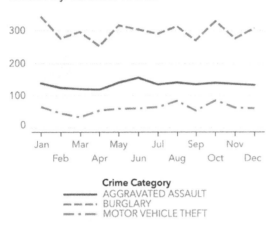

Crimes by Calendar Month

Crime Category
———— AGGRAVATED ASSAULT
– – – · BURGLARY
– · – · MOTOR VEHICLE THEFT

Figure 16: Chart from Figure 14, Using Both Color and Line Pattern to Distinguish Lines

Figure 14 shows a time series chart using color alone to convey meaning. Each line in the chart is color coded, and you must be able to perceive color to distinguish one line from another.

Figure 15 shows the same chart in gray scale. This is what the image looks like without any color. Note that it's essentially impossible to distinguish one line from another. This figure simulates the experience of someone with no color perception.

Figure 16 shows the same chart with both color and line patterns used to distinguish one line from another. This is the best of both worlds. People with good color perception can still use color to distinguish one line from another, while people with color deficient vision can still tell one line from another by using the pattern. As a bonus, we've also improved the usability of the chart for anyone who prints it on a black-and-white printer.

To achieve this effect of using both color and line pattern in line charts and time series charts, set the report-level option **Data element style rotation** to **Rotate all attributes**. Note that this option applies to SAS Visual Analytics 8.3 and later. SAS Visual Analytics 7.4 and later uses object-level options to achieve similar effects.

GEO MAP

The central object in the Geographic Area section of the example report is a Geo Map object. Geo maps are complex objects with many accessibility considerations. While it is possible to use geo maps in ways that are compliant with WCAG 2.0 AA, doing so limits the functionality of the geo maps. For example, as of the writing of this paper, any geo map that shows a background image, including the geo map used in the example report, does not comply with WCAG 2.0 AA. A reason for this non-compliance is insufficient contrast between various elements of the background (such as insufficient contrast of the text for place names against their background colors). There can be other reasons that geo maps are not compliant. Geo maps do not respect some accessibility settings such as dynamic text (increased text size) on iOS or the use of a high contrast report theme.

However, it is still possible to use geo maps in your report and maintain overall compliance for the report by presenting the same information in another type of object that is accessible. You can do this because WCAG 2.0 allows for inaccessible content if there is an accessible alternative representation of the same content.

The Geographic Area page of the example report shows information about the geographic distribution of police incidents in two forms: a geo map and a list table. The information in the list table essentially duplicates the information in the geo map. This is useful not only to people with disabilities, who might have an easier time accessing the information in list table form, but to people without disabilities as well. It allows everyone to answer questions such as, "which neighborhoods have the greatest number of crimes?"

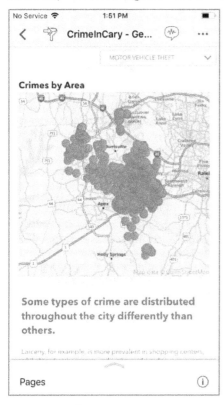

Figure 17: Crimes by Area Geo Map

Figure 18: Crimes by Area List Table

LIST TABLE

List tables comply with WCAG 2.0 AA. Other than avoiding certain options mentioned in the Universal Considerations section of this paper, there is nothing that you need to do to ensure that list tables remain compliant. In fact, list tables are a useful way to present information in an alternative, accessible form when you want to use an object that has accessibility issues, as in the geo map example shown above. You can use this same technique of duplicating information in a list table when you want to use other object types that are less accessible.

ACCESSIBILITY OF OTHER TYPES OF OBJECTS

The types of objects mentioned in this paper include excellent integrated accessibility such that you generally do not need to represent the same data in another more accessible form. If you create reports that include types of objects not mentioned in this paper or in the document *Creating Accessible Reports Using SAS® Visual Analytics 7.4*, you should consider those objects to be inaccessible. In this case, you should also include their content in another, more accessible form, such as a list table.

In future releases of SAS Visual Analytics, SAS plans to expand the set of known-accessible objects and publish updated guidance about creating accessible reports.

OBJECT NAMES OR TITLES

Give every object in your report either a meaningful visible title, or a meaningful object name. This is important because screen reader users rely on object names and titles to identify objects. As of the publication of this paper, VoiceOver identifies report objects in these ways:

- If there is a visible title for the object, VoiceOver announces the title.
- If there is no visible title for the object, VoiceOver announces the object name.

Meaningful names should convey the purpose of the object and the data that it presents. The names do not need to include the object type, because VoiceOver communicates the object type to screen reader users. The example report includes visible titles for most graph objects, such as Most Common Crimes and Crimes by Calendar Month. Objects that don't include a visible title include a meaningful object name.

SENSORY CHARACTERISTICS IN TEXT

Avoid using sensory characteristics such as shape, size, color, or position, as the sole identifying information in descriptive or instructional text within your report. Screen reader users and others might not have access to these characteristics. For example, suppose you included this description of a chart in a Text object (as illustrated in Figure 19):

"As you can see from the green line marked with dots and long dashes, some types of crime dip in the colder months of January, February and especially March."

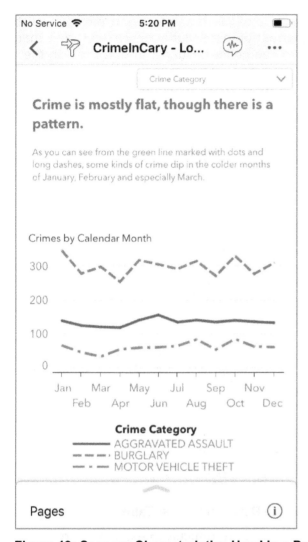

Figure 19: Sensory Characteristics Used in a Problematic Way

Even though people with color deficient vision can understand this description, it still presents a problem for screen reader users, who can only tell that a line called Motor Vehicle Theft exists. They cannot tell that the line is green, or that it is formed with dots and longer dashes. A better description would simply use the name of the line, or more generally, use the name of the element or object being referred to. It's okay to include sensory characteristics along with more accessible identifying information. For example, you can include text such as these examples:

- "As you can see in the Crimes Over Time chart on the left…"
- "…in the Motor Vehicle Theft line, shown in green, you'll notice a dip in March."

In both descriptions, the sensory characteristic supplements non-sensory identifying information.

INTERACTIONS

As of the publication of this paper, SAS Visual Analytics App for iOS does not supply information to VoiceOver users about interactions between objects. This can make it difficult for VoiceOver users to discover interactions such as filtering and linking. To work around this limitation, you can use a Text object to note and explain interactions between objects in your reports. For example, the Geographic Area section of the example report includes a list table that filters a geo map. The instructions in the text object include a note indicating that you can select an area listed in the table in order to see police incidents in that area on the map.

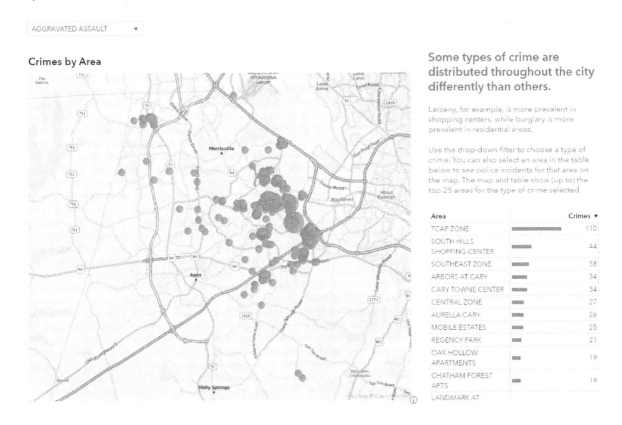

Figure 20: Text Instructions Identify Filtering Relationship Between the List Table and Geo Map

You should also avoid complex chains of interactions that are difficult to explain in order to make your reports easier for everyone to use, regardless of their ability.

DATA ELEMENT STYLE ROTATION

As mentioned in the section on Time Series Plots and Line Charts, to increase accessibility you should turn on the **Data Element Style Rotation** report-level option. This option causes certain chart types, including line charts, time series plots, scatter plots, and needle plots, to use either line pattern or point shapes to distinguish one group or measure from another. In the future, SAS plans to expand this option to cover more chart types.

AVOID FEATURES THAT DON'T COMPLY WITH WCAG 2.0 AA

As of the publication of this paper, these features do not comply with WCAG 2.0 AA and should be avoided:

- Display rules
- Brushing
- Overview axes
- Lattice columns and lattice rows
- Animation

- Reference lines

If you need to use one or more of these features, consider that section of your report to be inaccessible. Include the same information in a more accessible form elsewhere within your report.

CONCLUSION

By following the examples and suggestions in this paper, you can make your reports comply with WCAG 2.0 AA, which is the most widely used technical standard for digital accessibility. Complying with this standard not only helps your organization meet its legal or policy requirements, but also allows people with disabilities to access your reports. Compliance also makes your reports easier for everyone to use and understand, regardless of their abilities.

SAS is actively improving the accessibility of SAS Visual Analytics. The information in this paper is current as of the publication date. For the most up-to-date information on the accessibility of SAS Visual Analytics, see *Creating Accessible Reports Using SAS® Visual Analytics 7.4*. SAS also plans to publish a similar document for other recent versions of SAS Visual Analytics.

REFERENCES

Coyle, Cheryl, Mark Malek, Chelsea Mayse, Vaidehi Patil, Sierra Shell 2017. "Data Can Be Beautiful: Crafting a Compelling Story with SAS® Visual Analytics." *Proceedings of the SAS Global Forum 2017 Conference.* Cary, NC: SAS Institute Inc. Available at http://support.sas.com/resources/papers/proceedings17/SAS0545-2017.pdf.

Gabrielle, Bruce. "Why Tufte Is Flat-Out Wrong about Pie Charts." Available at http://speakingppt.com/why-tufte-is-flat-out-wrong-about-pie-charts/. Accessed March 19, 2019.

Mandavilli, Lavanya and Anand Chitale. 2016. "Carry-on Suitcases and Mobile Devices: Using SAS® Visual Analytics Designer for Creating Optimally Designed Reports for SAS® Mobile BI." *Proceedings of the SAS Global Forum 2016 Conference.* Cary, NC: SAS Institute Inc. Available at http://support.sas.com/resources/papers/proceedings16/SAS3802-2016.pdf.

SAS Institute, Inc. 2018. *Creating Accessible Reports Using SAS® Visual Analytics 7.4.* Cary, NC: SAS Institute Inc. Availablehttps://documentation.sas.com/?docsetId=vacar&docsetTarget=titlepage.htm&docsetVersion=7.4&locale=en. (accessed March 19, 2019)

"Police Incidents." Town of Cary, North Carolina. Available https://data.townofcary.org/explore/dataset/cpd-incidents/information/?disjunctive.crime_category&disjunctive.crime_type&disjunctive.crime_day&disjunctive.district&disjunctive.offensecategory&disjunctive.violentproperty&disjunctive.total_incidents. Accessed on February 26, 2019.

"Understanding WCAG 2.0." W3C. Available https://www.w3.org/TR/UNDERSTANDING-WCAG20/Overview.html. Accessed on March 19, 2019.

RECOMMENDED READING

SAS Institute, Inc. 2018. *Creating Accessible Reports Using SAS® Visual Analytics 7.4*. Cary, NC: SAS Institute Inc. Available https://documentation.sas.com/?docsetId=vacar&docsetTarget=titlepage.htm&docsetVersion=7.4&locale=en. (accessed March 19, 2019)

"SAS Accessibility" YouTube. Available https://www.youtube.com/playlist?list=PLVBcK_IpFVi9kCxPXz4dd1HO5x_yLLEHJ. Accessed on March 20, 2019.

SAS Institute Inc. 2019. *SAS Visual Analytics App for iOS: Accessibility Features*. Cary, NC: SAS Institute Inc. Available https://documentation.sas.com/?cdcId=bivwrcdc&cdcVersion=8.36&docsetId=bivwra11y&docsetTarget=n1vdm3jhgm14oln12uuvdmuuq0sl.htm&locale=en. (accessed March 20, 2019)

SAS Institute Inc. 2018. *Accessibility Features of SAS Visual Analytics 7.4*. Cary, NC: SAS Institute Inc. Available http://support.sas.com/documentation/prod-p/va/7.4/en/HTML/vaa11y.htm. (accessed March 20, 2019)

SAS Institute Inc. 2018. *SAS Visual Analytics 8.3: Accessibility Features*. Cary, NC: SAS Institute Inc. Available https://documentation.sas.com/?docsetId=vaa11y&docsetTarget=p1lt5lhiixhrnwn1romejo5znkq7.htm&docsetVersion=8.3&locale=en. (accessed March 20, 2019)

CONTACT INFORMATION

Your comments and questions are valued and encouraged. Contact the author at:

Jesse Sookne
SAS Institute Inc.
jesse.sookne@sas.com

Mastering Parameters in SAS® Visual Analytics

Stu Sztukowski, SAS Institute Inc.

ABSTRACT

SAS® Visual Analytics provides simple, straight-forward filtering mechanisms that work right out of the box with almost no configuration needed: drop a control (filter) into a report and assign a variable role to it. It's easy, quick, and satisfies most UI requirements for users. When used on their own, report controls only filter other objects and do not provide any additional information to you, the designer. For example, if a user selects a filter, it might be helpful to know:

- What filter did they select?
- What value or values does the filter hold?
- Can I use the value they selected in calculated variables?

Visual Analytics allows you to answer these questions through special variables called parameters.

Parameters are data set independent dynamic variables in Visual Analytics that can be added to report controls to store user-selected value(s) of lists, buttons, sliders, and other controls into a variable or group of variables. Often underused, parameters provide you with a powerful level of control over the report.

INTRODUCTION

There are three types of parameters available in Visual Analytics:

1. Character
2. Numeric
3. Date/datetime

The types of values that a parameter will accept are self-explanatory. Character parameters can only accept character values, numeric parameters can only accept numeric values, and date/datetime parameters can only accept date or datetime values.

Parameters are like categorical, measure, or datetime variables. They work with the same values, can be used in calculated variables, and can be assigned to controls. There are two differentiating factors that make them such powerful assets in a report:

1. They are data set agnostic: parameters are independent of report data sets
2. They are dynamic: they change values as users interact with them

When you create a parameter, it is tied solely to the report and not any one data set, unlike a calculated variable, which can only be used within the data set in which it was created. Due to this data set independence, parameters require some sort of input to give them a value. This is either a static value that you decide, or a dynamic value that is populated from a control in the report.

WHAT IS A PARAMETER, ANYWAY?

A parameter is defined as "a variable whose value can be changed and that can be referenced by other report objects." What makes parameters unique from other variables is that they can be changed *by the user* using report controls. One way to think of a parameter is like a large drink jar. You can fill it with any liquids that you like: water, juice, wine, and so on. The jar will remain filled with your beverage of choice until you decide to change it, whether you empty it or switch it with another drink.

Figure 1. Parameters can be thought of as a container that holds something.

For those with SAS programming experience, think of a parameter like a macro variable. On its own, a macro variable has no value unless it is either given an initial value or changed at another time. For example, the consider the statement below:

```
%global macvar;
```

The macro variable macvar is created and available for use. By default, its value is simply missing. macvar can hold a value by assigning one to it.

```
%let macvar = 1;
```

macvar now has a value of 1 and can be used in other calculations. It will always hold this value until you change it. Throughout your program, macvar is available to store values as you'd like. Like parameters, macro variables require something else to change its default value.

The best way to learn how to use parameters is by example. This paper will provide five examples of using parameters to enhance both Visual Analytics 7.4 and 8.2+ reports:

1. Dynamic ranks
2. Dynamic variables
3. Dynamic titles
4. Simple "What-If" calculators
5. Dynamic dates for drop-down list filters

All examples in this paper are accompanied by sample reports and data for Visual Analytics 7.4, 8.2, and 8.3.1.

DYNAMIC RANKS

For many business decisions, knowing the highest and lowest values in a category are important, especially if there are thousands of unique values. For example, a CEO might want to know the top 10 most profitable products that his or her company produces. Visual Analytics gives you the ability to apply a rank to a categorical variable for an object. Typically, this is a static value set by you, the designer. If you want to change it, you need to re-open the report in Designer Mode, change the value, and save it. With parameters, you can skip those steps and allow users to decide which top *x* or *x%* of a category to show.

Figure 2. Applying a rank to a category (7.4).

Figure 3. Applying a rank to a category (8.2+).

Suppose you are interested in buying a car. It needs to be fast – really fast. *sashelp.cars* is a data set conveniently located in your SASHELP directory that has vehicle statistics, and you also have access to Visual Analytics. You load *sashelp.cars* into Visual Analytics and create the bar chart in Figure 4 that shows the average horsepower by model.

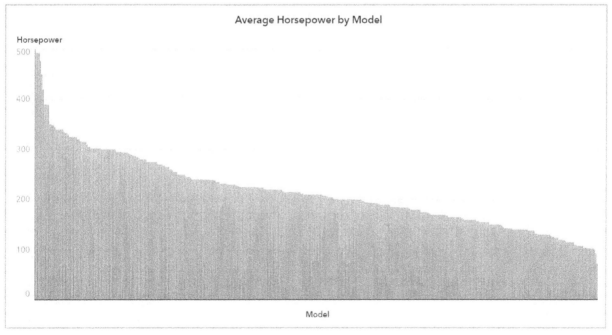

Figure 4. Bar chart of Horsepower by Model.

Yikes! That's a lot of cars. To make this easier to see, you'd like to be able to rank the top *x* models by horsepower and give yourself the flexibility to change that value on the fly.

STEPS TO CREATE EXAMPLE REPORT

1. Load *sashelp.cars* as a promoted CAS table, or into LASR.
2. Drag a slider control anywhere into the report and leave it without any roles.
3. Create a bar chart and set the roles as follows:
   a. **Category:** *Model*
   b. **Measures:** *Horsepower* with an aggregation of *average*
4. Click on the bar chart and select the "Ranks" option. If this is not visible in Visual Analytics 7.4, click ⏷ on the right-hand corner of the screen and select ⠿ Ranks
5. In the drop-down list of the *Ranks* option menu, select *Model* and click *Add Rank*.
6. In the *By:* drop-down list, select *Horsepower*.
7. Uncheck *Ties* and *All Other*.

CREATING YOUR FIRST PARAMETER

There is an additional option to use a parameter under the *Count* option. Instead of forcing a static value of 10 for the *Top Makes by Horsepower*, you can take advantage of the *Parameter* option to let the user decide the top number of car makes by horsepower they would like to see. To use this, you first need to create a numeric parameter. This can be done in two different ways depending on your version of Visual Analytics.

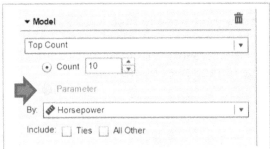

Figure 5. Parameter Option for Ranks (7.4).

Figure 6. Parameter Option for Ranks (8.2+).

Visual Analytics 7.4

On the left side of the page, click ⏷ , and create a new numeric parameter.

Visual Analytics 8.2+

You can create a new parameter by clicking ✚ New data item in the *Data* tab on the left-hand side of the screen and selecting 🅧 Parameter...; however, Visual Analytics 8.2+ gives you a shortcut to create a parameter if it does not yet exist in the *Ranks* tab. Under *Count:,* select the drop-down menu and click *New parameter...*

Set the options in Table 1 for the parameter:

Parameter Name	Min	Max	Current Value	Format	Decimals
User Rank	1	25	10	Float	0

Table 1. Options for User Rank parameter.

USING THE PARAMETER

Click on the slider you added to the report and add your new parameter to the *parameter* role. In the *Ranks* tab of your bar chart, ensure that your parameter is selected under the *Count* option.

Figure 7. Parameter Count (7.4).   **Figure 8. Parameter Count (8.2+).**

Save, and then switch back to the report viewer and try moving the slider like in Figure 9.

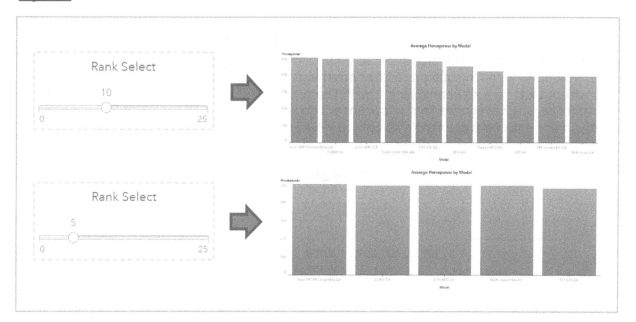

Figure 9. Using a slider with a parameter to control the top values displayed in a bar chart.

Thanks to your report, you've narrowed down the top 10 fastest vehicles on the market. Your significant other wanted to see the top 20, and you were able to show that easily thanks to your filter. After reviewing your options, you decide that a Dodge Viper might not be a good investment and settle on a gently used Nissan Sentra instead.

DYNAMIC VARIABLES

Within 500-1000ms of their first impression, people form their initial opinions of a person, and user interfaces are not much different. If the initial look of an interface is cluttered and full of graphs, it can quickly drive a user away. When users want to see multiple identical graphs for different variables in a single report, the report space can become overcrowded with stacked containers, tabs, and duplicated graphs whose only differences are the variables being displayed. If this happens, the user can feel lost or confused as to what they might be looking at or where to find the information that they want. This compounds further when interactions are added between various graphs in stacked containers.

A trick for giving users more flexibility to see data of interest without overcrowding a report is by allowing the user to select a variable to display in a graph using a button. If the button were to dynamically change the variable being shown, then more information can be displayed on a page while introducing minimal clutter. Parameters give you this flexibility.

CREATING A UTILITY DATA SET

When you create a button, you can assign an optional character parameter to it. Unlike numeric or date parameters, character parameters cannot be assigned a set of static values. They can only hold the value of a pre-existing categorical variable that is assigned to the button. If you add a parameter to a button without adding a categorical data item, the button will not function. This same rule applies to drop-down menus and lists.

For example, using *sashelp.cars*, suppose you want to have a bar chart where users can choose to display the average City MPG or Highway MPG by Make via a button (Figure 10).

Figure 10. Variable selection button.

Buttons need a category to give them text since their primary function is for filtering. In this case, you don't want the button to filter anything. You need to do a trick to give the button text without letting it filter anything else in the report. A set of utility data sets will allow you to make any categories that you want without interacting with report objects or each other. Utility data sets are simple to create in SAS:

```
data va_dummy_data_body;
    do dummy_data_body = 1 to 25;
        output;
    end;
run;

data va_dummy_data_local;
    do dummy_data_local = 1 to 25;
        output;
    end;
run;

data va_dummy_data_global;
    do dummy_data_global = 1 to 25;
        output;
    end;
run;
```

Figure 11. Creating utility data sets using SAS.

Three data sets are created, all with different names and variables to prevent Visual Analytics from automatically assigning variable mappings. If Visual Analytics asks you to assign variable mappings for your utility data sets, do not assign them. Depending on where you place your controls, you'll want to use a data set in a specific location within the report. This keeps the controls independent of each other and prevents any unintended filtering.

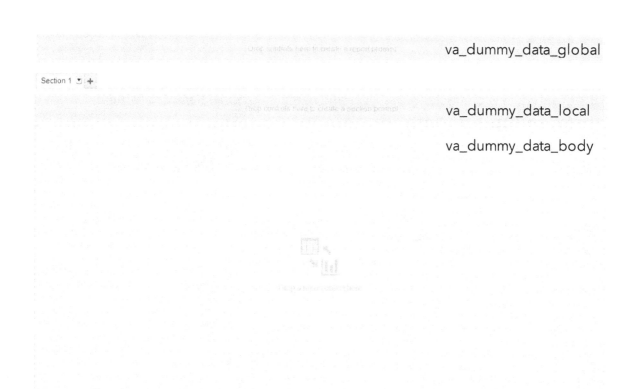

Section 1 ▾ ✚

va_dummy_data_global

va_dummy_data_local

va_dummy_data_body

Figure 12. Where to use utility data sets in Visual Analytics report objects.

USING THE UTILITY DATA SET WITH A PARAMETER

For this example, drag a button to the body of the report, place it under an *Average MPG by Make* bar chart, and set it as *required*. Next, perform the following steps:

1. Add the utility data set *va_dummy_data_body* to your report.
2. Right-click the variable *dummy_data_body*, click *New Custom Category...*, and name it *Variable Select* ([Figure 13](#)).
3. Create a new group called *MPG (City)* and add a value to it.
4. Group the remaining values as *MPG (Highway)*.

Figure 13. Creating button text using values of *dummy_data_body*.

7

5. Give *Variable Select* a role in the button.

6. Create a new character parameter and name it *Variable Select Parameter*.

7. Add *Variable Select Parameter* as a role in the button.

Great! You have a button with a parameter. Now you need to make the parameter do something. At the moment, it only takes on the value of whatever is selected on the button.

PUTTING THE PARAMETER TO WORK

You now have everything that you need to create a dynamically changing variable. The button logic is basic: if the user selects *MPG (City)*, you want to display values of *MPG (City)*. Otherwise, you want to display the *MPG (Highway)* variable. The value of the parameter tells you what the user has selected. Follow the next steps to finish the exercise.

1. Select the *cars* data set and create a new calculated variable named *MPG* with an aggregation of *average*.

2. Select the *text* tab and add the following code:

```
if(upcase('Variable Select Parameter'p) = 'MPG (CITY)')
return 'MPG (City)'n
    else 'MPG (Highway)'n
```

3. Add your newly created *MPG* variable to the bar chart.

4. Click the button and observe the effects on the graph.

Note that the variable name *MPG* is always static because Visual Analytics does not support dynamic variable names as of this paper. The user only knows what is being displayed from the highlighted button. In reports where space is at a premium and controls are hidden in prompt containers, dynamic titles can help users know what is being shown.

DYNAMIC TITLES AND TEXT REPORTS

If you have dynamic variables or filters inside of a prompt container, users might be wondering which variables are being displayed or which filters are being applied. For example, selected values within prompt containers are hidden unless the user happens to click ⓘ on an individual object to see if any filters are applied.

Figure 14. Object filter information displayed after clicking ⓘ

Instead, you can bring these filter values to the attention of the viewer at the top of the page by associating parameters with each report control and using them within a text box.

CREATING DYNAMIC TITLES FROM PARAMETERS

Expanding on the previous example, add the following filters to the report:

1. Add three required list controls in a prompt container: *DriveTrain, Type,* and *Origin.*

2. Create three character parameters and add each parameter to a report control (Figure 15).

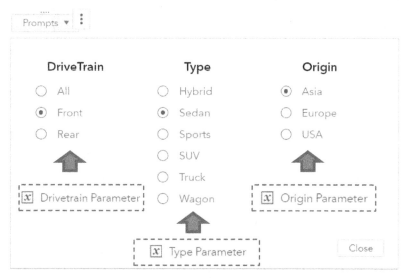

Figure 15. Adding three new parameters to report controls.

You want to create some descriptive text that tells the user about the filters selected. For example, if the user selects front wheel drive Asian sedans, you might want something at the top of the report that says:

Average MPG (Highway) of Front Wheel Drive Sedans made in Asia

To do this, create a new text box at the top of your report and begin entering the title. For each part of the title that is dynamic, add the desired parameter to the text box.

Figure 16. Incorporating parameters as dynamic text into a text box.

Continue entering your title and adding parameters as needed until your title is complete.

Average {Variable Select} of {Drivetrain Parameter} Wheel Drive {Type Parameter}s made in {Origin Parameter}

Figure 17. How the dynamic text box should look in Text Box Edit Mode.

Click through values in the controls within the prompt container and watch the title dynamically change.

DYNAMIC TEXT REPORTS

The dynamic title concept can be further expanded to full text reports that change dynamically based on filter values. Sometimes people like a good executive summary rather than graphs, and those can be tedious to enter on a regular basis. You can save yourself time by having Visual Analytics crunch the numbers and have the text already prepared for you. Parameters and measures can live together harmoniously in text boxes for this purpose.

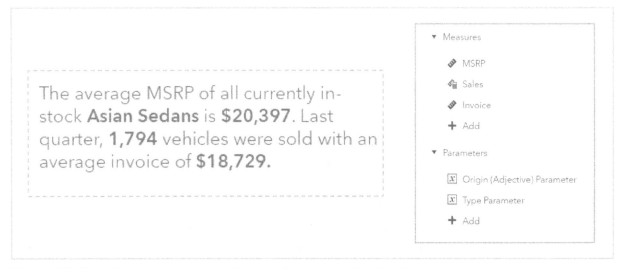

Figure 18. Combining measures and parameters to create a text summary.

SIMPLE WHAT-IF CALCULATORS

When reports are flexible and interactive, users become more interested and can get greater value out of them. One effective way is by creating simple calculators out of report controls that can let users make assumption-based scenarios. For example, a user can adjust values of a slider to see how a bank loan is affected by different interest rates. These types of calculators give users a wide range of assumption-based scenarios that can help them narrow down areas of focus and interest.

Continuing to expand on the report you made from Dynamic Ranks, you've managed to convince your significant other to buy a high horsepower car, but only under the condition that you also get something fuel efficient to offset your carbon footprint. Recall that you settled with a used Nissan Sentra, but you *also* went out and leased a 2020 BMW M340i. You're about to go on your yearly three-week trip to visit your in-laws in Hays, Kansas. It's a long drive from Raleigh, North Carolina, and you'd like to estimate out how much it would cost you in fuel between the two vehicles.

You have a few different routes in mind that can make the trip more interesting. If you take the BMW, you've got nearly 400 horsepower at the command of your right foot, so you'll want to take a route that includes the Tail of the Dragon: one of the most famous curvy roads sought after by motorcyclists and car enthusiasts. If you take the Sentra, you'll want to drive on the straightest, flattest interstate you can find. To make it easier to review these different ideas, you want to add a tab to your Visual Analytics report with a fuel cost calculator to help estimate how much it will cost you to drive using various routes that you come up with.

To figure this out, you need to know a few things:

- Total distance
- % of total distance driven on the highway
- City MPG of your vehicle
- Highway MPG of your vehicle
- Average cost of fuel

Your desired metrics are:

- Gallons of fuel consumed
- Total cost of fuel

The two output metrics are based on formulas in Table 2:

Gallons of Fuel Consumed	$\dfrac{Distance_{highway}}{MPG_{highway}} + \dfrac{Distance_{city}}{MPG_{city}}$
Fuel Cost	$Gallons\ of\ Fuel\ Consumed * Avg\ Fuel\ Cost\ per\ Gallon$

Table 2. Output formulas

The metrics won't tell you precisely how much you'll spend on fuel, but it's in the ballpark and is a starting point to decide which car to take. You want to be able to use some report controls to be able to vary these values and see how they affect your output metrics.

Remember that parameters can be used in calculated items, and only measures or categories can be displayed in most report objects. Since you can create your formulas as calculated items in any data set, the most efficient way to calculate them is by using the smallest data set possible. At 25 observations, *va_dummy_data_body* is a good option. Note that in Visual Analytics, a calculated item is applied to every row. Since you have 25 rows in *va_dummy_data_body*, your formula will be repeated 25 times. Changing the aggregation method from *sum* to *average* will return the correct value.

STEPS TO CREATE REPORT

1. Create five new numeric parameters with the options in Table 3:

Parameter Name	Min	Max	Current Value	Format	Decimals
Total Distance	0	10,000	1	Comma	0
% Highway Miles	0	1	1	Percent	0
City MPG	0	75	1	Best	0
Highway MPG	0	75	1	Best	0
Avg Fuel Cost	0	5	1	Dollar	2

Table 3. Parameter options for calculator inputs.

2. Create two new calculated measures in *va_dummy_data_body* with an aggregation of *average*.

    a. **Gallons**

```
('Total Distance'p * '% Highway Miles Parameter'p) / 'Highway MPG
Parameter'p

+

('Total Distance Parameter'p * (1 - '% Highway Miles Parameter'p) ) /
'City MPG Parameter'p
```

    b. **Fuel Cost**

```
'Gallons'n * 'Price/Gallon Parameter'p
```

3. Add report controls to the body of your report such as those in <u>Figure 19</u> and <u>Figure 20</u>, and attach the appropriate parameters to them; these will be the values you can adjust for your calculator.

4. Add objects to visualize the *Gallons* and *Fuel Cost* measures.

USING THE CALCULATOR

It's 1,334 miles one way from Raleigh, NC to Hays, Kansas. You estimate that you'll be on the highway about 75% of the time, and you *really* want to take the BMW. Your 2020 M340i gets an average City and Highway MPG of 20 and 30, respectively. Since it has a high-performance turbocharged engine, you're stuck with using premium 93 at an average of $2.80 per gallon.

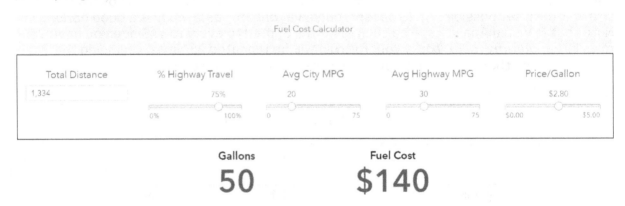

Figure 19. Estimated fuel cost to drive a 2020 BMW M340i from Raleigh, NC to Hays, Kansas.

Next, you look at the humble 2017 Nissan Sentra. While less fun, it is more economical. The Sentra gets 29 city/37 highway MPG and only needs to use 87 at the pump, costing an average of $2.21/gallon.

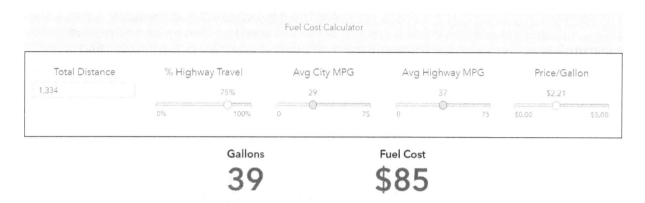

Figure 20. Estimated fuel cost to drive a 2017 Nissan Sentra from Raleigh, NC to Hays, Kansas.

Using the Sentra, you'll save around $110 on fuel costs round-trip. In the end, you take the Sentra since the lease on your BMW only lets you drive 12,000 miles per year anyway.

DYNAMIC MAXIMUMS WITH DROP-DOWN LISTS

In forecasting, being able to review how forecasts change over time is paramount to ensuring quality forecasts. Visual Analytics makes it easy to review forecast start dates over time. With wide, regular time intervals, sliders are a great option to easily let users explore data. For infrequent or granular time intervals, drop-down lists are a better option. A drawback to using drop-down lists is the inability to have a dynamic maximum value (as of this report). Using parameters, you can add that functionality.

LIMITATIONS OF SLIDERS

In early versions of Visual Analytics, the value of a slider last saved in Designer mode was the default value every time the report was opened. For example, consider a forecast report that updates monthly. A user can use a slider to move back and forth between forecast start dates to review historical forecasts. When the report is first created, the forecast start date is set to its maximum by the designer. The next month the forecast updates, the forecast start date in the report remains at the previous value.

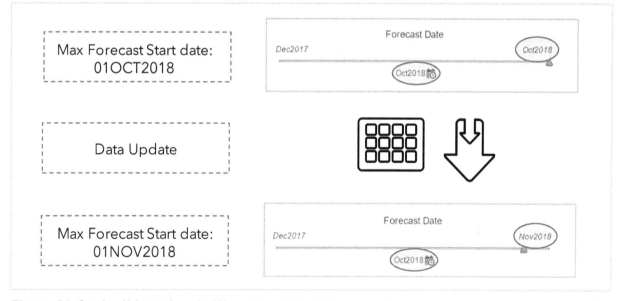

Figure 21. Static slider values in Visual Analytics 7.3 and earlier.

The solution was to open the report every time the data updated and manually change the slider, and then resave it. Versions 7.4 and 8.x introduced the "Set value to dynamic minimum" and "Set value to dynamic maximum" options for sliders to resolve this issue.

☐ Set value to dynamic minimum

☐ Set value to dynamic maximum

Figure 22. Dynamic slider minimums/maximums in Visual Analytics 7.4 and 8.x

Sliders increment in equal, standard time intervals, making them great for data that is updated on a regular wide time interval, such as weekly, monthly, yearly, and so on. Unfortunately, data is not always updated regularly, nor is it always at such a wide interval. Sliders can be difficult to use with dense data containing granular time periods such as day and hour. Also, any time gaps within the data are still able to be selected by the user, allowing users to select any invalid dates that exist. For example, if a forecast updates every *two* months rather than every month, selecting every other month on the slider will create errors in the report.

Source Data		Forecast Start Date
Forecast_Start_Date	...	Oct2018
01SEP2018	...	Dec2017 ——— Nov2018
...	...	⬇
01NOV2018	...	⚠
...	...	The filter resulted in an empty set of data.

Figure 23. An invalid filter value can still be selected with a slider.

Sliders include all possible dates between a range, which can make it ambiguous as to which forecast dates are valid or invalid. One solution would be to use a drop-down menu, which will show the user only valid values; however, there is no built-in option for a dynamic minimum or maximum value, bringing you back to the original problem. With some minor source data changes and with parameters, you can add this functionality.

ADDING DYNAMIC MAXIMUM FUNCTIONALITY TO DROP-DOWN LISTS

There are three steps to add dynamic maximums to drop-down menus:

1. Create a binary flag in your data identifying the maximum forecast start date.
2. Add a date parameter to the drop-down menu.
3. Add logic to every report object on the page to display the maximum forecast date when nothing is selected in the drop-down list.

Step 1: Add a Forecast Start Date Flag

You will need to know which forecast start date is the most current. One way is to add a binary flag whenever the data is updated. An example of this is shown below.

```
        /* Read in current forecast and add in a forecast start date. */
        data current_forecast;
            set outfor;

            forecast_start_date = today();
        run;

        /* Append the current forecast to all previous forecasts.
           Add a flag to tell us when the date of forecast is the most recent */
        data all_forecasts;
            set previous_forecasts
                current_forecast
                ;

            flag_max_forecast_start_date = (forecast_start_date = today() );
        run;
```

forecast_start_date	flag_max_forecast_start_date	...
01JAN2008	0	...
...	...	...
01OCT2018	0	...
01NOV2018	1	...

Figure 24. Creating a binary flag to identify the most recent forecast start date.

Step 2: Create a Date Parameter

Create a new date parameter and add it to your drop-down list. Give it a minimum value at least as low as the earliest forecast date, and a maximum value well above your maximum forecast date. Set the current value to any value.

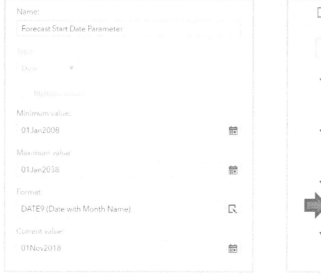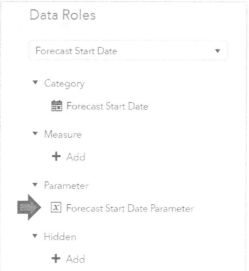

Figure 25. Creating a date parameter and adding it to a drop-down list.

15

Step 3: Add Object Filter Logic

For every object on the page affected by the drop-down list, add the filter in Figure 26:

```
if(missing('Forecast Start Date Parameter'p) )
    return 'flag_max_forecast_start_date'n = 1
            else 1=1
```

Figure 26. Object filter to force the maximum forecast date to display when no filter is selected.

The normal behavior of clearing a filter is to show every value. Now if you clear all filters in your forecast start date, it will only show the most recent valid forecast date.

HOW IT WORKS

When the drop-down list has no selection, the value of *Forecast Start Date Parameter* is missing. This is the only time the parameter will have a missing value. When it has a missing value, you want all objects on the page to filter to the most recent forecast start date: that is, when `'flag_max_forecast_start_date'n = 1`.

You don't want the object filter to do anything else when a forecast start date is selected. In Visual Analytics, if/then logic requires an `else` condition. To get around this, you can return an always-true condition such as 1=1. This makes the `else` statement do nothing, preventing any additional filtering at the object-level.

In other words, when you don't select a forecast start date, the object filter returns the most recent forecast start date. When you do select a forecast start date, the object filter does nothing. Table 4 shows how this logic is applied.

Drop-down List	Parameter Value	Report Control	Object Filter
Forecast Start Date ▼	(missing)	None	'flag_max_forecast_start_date'n = 1
Oct2018 ▼	'01OCT2018'd	'01OCT2018'd	None

Table 4. Drop-down list filter and object filter behavior.

If you are using Visual Analytics 8.3+, the process of creating individual object filters is greatly simplified thanks to the Common Filters feature. For more information, see Using Common Filters in the Visual Analytics users guide.

FINALIZING YOUR REPORT

Adding a dynamic title showing the selected forecast date in big, bold text is a good way to improve your report. You might be tempted to use the value of the parameter, but that won't be helpful this time. If the parameter is put into a text box, it will show <No item selected> until a forecast start date is selected.

A workaround is to create two new calculated measures that get the month and year from the forecast start date and set their aggregation to average. An example report of everything put together is shown in Figure 27.

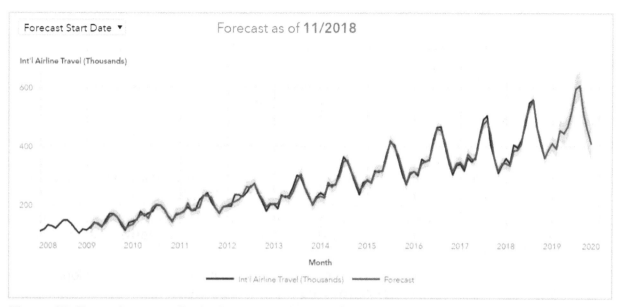

Figure 27. Example report displaying user-selectable forecast start dates.

A NOTE ON MULTI-VALUE PARAMETERS

Parameters can support holding multiple values, such as in multi-selection list controls. When using parameters in this way, the number of available functions that can act on them is limited. Only aggregation functions might act on numeric list parameters, and only string list functions might act on character/date list parameters. For example, consider the multi-valued parameters in Table 5:

'Char List'p	✗ if('Char List'p = 'DOG' OR 'Char List'p = 'CAT')
DOG,CAT,BIRD	✓ if('Char List'p IN('DOG', 'CAT'))
'Num List'p	✗ if('Num List'p)) = 1
1,2,3	✓ if(max('parameter 1'p)) = 1

Table 5. Example of using multi-valued parameters.

For more information about multi-valued parameters, see the SAS Help Documentation on Parameters.

CONCLUSION

Parameters are powerful tools in Visual Analytics that vastly expand what is possible within a report. The five examples presented in this white paper were selected to help you understand effective ways in which parameters can interact with a report. There are many other ways parameters can be used outside the scope of this paper. For example, if you are savvy with custom polygons in Visual Analytics, you can create a special polygon data set that holds multiple layers that can be selected by using parameters for dynamic geographic variables. Another example would be using parameters to feed inputs into Visual Statistics objects to vary forecast inputs, regression models, decision trees, and more. By mastering parameters, your report will become more flexible and feature-rich, allowing you to reach a wider audience who can get the information they need from fewer, simpler tabs.

REFERENCES

SAS® Institute. "Working with Parameters in Reports." February 21, 2019. Available at https://documentation.sas.com/?docsetId=vareportdata&docsetTarget=n1wv50n60ccq86n1 nzp6zat1wj64.htm&docsetVersion=8.3&locale=en

First Impressions: Making Up Your Mind After a 100-ms Exposure to a Face.
J Willis-A Todorov - https://www.ncbi.nlm.nih.gov/pubmed/16866745

ACKNOWLEDGMENTS

Thank you to my colleagues Kevin Baughman and Ryan Story for your inspiration to write this report. You are brilliant analysts who I am proud to work with.

Thank you to my mentor, Jared Peterson, who encouraged me to write my first white paper, and for always trying to get me to push myself further. You are a phenomenal leader and role model who I highly look up to.

Thank you to my manager, Ned Maran, who has supported my professional development and growth since day one. This report would not have been possible without your support.

RECOMMENDED READING

SAS® Visual Analytics 8.3 Documentation: Working with Report Data
https://documentation.sas.com/?docsetId=vareportdata&docsetTarget=titlepage.htm&docs etVersion=8.3&locale=en

Using Parameters in SAS® Visual Analytics
https://blogs.sas.com/content/sgf/2015/01/29/using-parameters-in-sas-visual-analytics/

CONTACT INFORMATION

Your comments and questions are valued and encouraged. Contact the author at:

Robert (Stu) Sztukowski
SAS Institute Inc
(919) 531-3238
Stu.Sztukowski@sas.com
https://www.linkedin.com/in/StatsGuy

Paper SAS3455-2019

Open Visualization with SAS® Viya® and Python

Joe Indelicato, SAS Institute Inc.

ABSTRACT

As SAS® continues to push boundaries with its cloud-based analytics ecosystem, SAS® Viya®, SAS also continues to break new ground as well! With a new initiative to become more open to developers via a robust API, and current integration with the Python package known as SWAT (Scripting Wrapper for Analytics Transfer), there are opportunities to take your in-house data science initiatives to a higher level. This session looks at incorporating open-source graphing techniques, specifically Python's matplotlib integrated with the popular D3 visualization framework, to generate interactive plots that can spur discovery of the story your data is trying to tell you. We work through some traditional statistical programming examples via calls in Jupyter Notebook to SAS Viya. Finally, within Jupyter, we convert our static graphs into dynamic graphs using mpld3, an open-source Python library that marries D3 to Python.

INTRODUCTION

With the release of SAS Viya, SAS continues its commitment to being a company of open-source inclusiveness. SAS has now adopted a culture that does not require SAS code to be written and called from within a SAS environment. SAS now has the ability to be called as a package and to be included in the most popular open-source languages. This approach has revolutionized commercial and open-source interoperability.

In this paper we are going to look at the use of Python, one of the most popular open-source programming languages. We are also going to examine how using Jupyter Notebook as an integrated development environment (IDE) can enable us to build interactive connections between the two frameworks. This synergy will give us the ability to harness the algorithms and the computing power of SAS, marry it to the data set standardization of Pandas, and ultimately create beautiful new graphs in Python with the D3 library.

To demonstrate the flexibility of this relationship, we will further explore the ability to combine mpld3 as a wrapper that allows Python to dynamically produce D3 charts. The programming examples contained in this paper will be demonstrated in both SAS code and in Python.

SAS SWAT

At the foundation of SAS Viya, is the SAS Cloud Analytic Services Engine, which is more commonly referred to as CAS. Requests to CAS are made from executables that SAS defines as actions. These actions function as an interface into the CAS server. Actions come in many different flavors. Some offer the ability to execute data integration tasks, while others give access to the analytic toolset upon which SAS has built its reputation. When we speak about Python, we are talking about a specific CAS action, SAS SWAT. SWAT enables Python to communicate with SAS CAS, which becomes useful when we encounter issues that comes from working inside of Python data size constraints. With the SWAT package, you can load and analyze data sets of any size on your desktop or the cloud. Because CAS can be used in any of these environments, it enables you to analyze extremely large data sets with flexible and scalable processing power while still retaining the simplicity of Python.

SAS takes Python integration a step further by leveraging the capability of returning data structures that are consumable by the popular Python pandas package. This allows the Python user the ability to combine the returned data with other data, or to pass the returned data through to other operations within Python, such as visualizations.

CAS

When data objects are returned from a SWAT call, these objects are returned as a CASTable. A CASTable is an in-memory table that can be consumable as a DataFrame by a SAS CASResults object. Although these two classes are independent of each other, they work together to produce DataFrame results.

Let's look at a quick example of this processing. Figure 1 shows how Python first imports a SAS library, and then show how data is pulled from a source and then loaded into a CASTable and a CASResult object.

```
In [15]:  import swat

In [24]:  s = swat.CAS host, port, userid, password

In [25]:  print(s)
```

Figure 1. Data Import and Load

The code in Figure 1 builds the connection back to SAS. SWAT is the package that allows all the actions from inside of CAS to be called.

We then need to upload the data file into CAS, as shown in Figure 2.

f

```
In [27]:  titanic3 = s.CASTable("titanic3", replace=True)

In [28]:  s.upload_file('http://biostat.mc.vanderbilt.edu/wiki/pub/Main/DataSets/titanic3.csv', casout=titanic3)
```

Figure 2. Upload Data File to CAS

The code in Figure 2 creates an in-memory table called "titanic3". In this case we are pulling in an external file into CAS and making that table available to us in memory.

Now that we have a data set in CAS, let's look at the columnar description of the table. To do that we execute a COLUMNINFO call, as shown in Figure 3.

```
In [52]:  titanic3.table.columnInfo()
```

Out[52]: § ColumnInfo

	Column	ID	Type	RawLength	FormattedLength	NFL	NFD
0	pclass	1	double	8	12	0	0
1	survived	2	double	8	12	0	0
2	name	3	varchar	82	82	0	0
3	sex	4	varchar	6	6	0	0
4	age	5	double	8	12	0	0
5	sibsp	6	double	8	12	0	0
6	parch	7	double	8	12	0	0
7	ticket	8	varchar	18	18	0	0
8	fare	9	double	8	12	0	0
9	cabin	10	varchar	15	15	0	0
10	embarked	11	varchar	1	1	0	0
11	boat	12	varchar	7	7	0	0
12	body	13	double	8	12	0	0
13	home.dest	14	varchar	50	50	0	0

elapsed 0.0101s · user 0.00959s · sys 0.00186s · mem 1.69MB

Figure 3. COLUMNINFO Call

We are now able to view the properties of the CASTable that we just created. You can see that the variable types are all SAS compatible. This is because the data was uploaded through the CAS and inherits SAS data types.

Let's now examine a summary of the data that we imported. You will note that this data in Figure 4 comes from the details of the passengers on the ill-fated voyage of the Titanic.

```
In [53]:  summaryResults = titanic3.simple.summary()

In [54]:  display(summaryResults.Summary[['Column', 'Min', 'Max', 'N', 'NMiss', 'Mean', 'Sum', 'Std', 'StdErr']])
```

Descriptive Statistics for TITANIC3

	Column	Min	Max	N	NMiss	Mean	Sum	Std	StdErr
0	pclass	1.00	3.0000	1309.0	0.0	2.294882	3004.0000	0.837836	0.023157
1	survived	0.00	1.0000	1309.0	0.0	0.381971	500.0000	0.486055	0.013434
2	age	0.17	80.0000	1046.0	263.0	29.881138	31255.6700	14.413493	0.445660
3	sibsp	0.00	8.0000	1309.0	0.0	0.498854	653.0000	1.041658	0.028791
4	parch	0.00	9.0000	1309.0	0.0	0.385027	504.0000	0.865560	0.023924
5	fare	0.00	512.3292	1308.0	1.0	33.295479	43550.4869	51.758668	1.431130
6	body	1.00	328.0000	121.0	1188.0	160.809917	19458.0000	97.696922	8.881538

Figure 4. Data Summary

By making a call to the SUMMARY procedure, we can see a summary of the data in the CASTable.

If we want to examine the data grouped by the passengers that survived and the passengers that perished, we use BYGROUP calls to group the data.

```
In [55]:  import matplotlib.pyplot as plt
          from IPython.core.display import display, HTML
          %matplotlib inline
```

```
In [56]:  titanic3.computedVars = ["deck"]                          # 1
          titanic3.computedVarsProgram = \
              "if cabin ne '' then deck = ksubstr(cabin,1,1); else deck = '';"

          numeric=['pclass', 'survived', 'age', 'sibsp', 'parch', 'fare']

          # Remove boat and body because they are proxies for survived
          # Remove ticket and cabin. Use the computed column, deck, instead.
          char = ['sex', 'deck', 'embarked', 'home.dest']

          all = numeric + char
```

```
In [57]:  # numeric was defined earlier
          results = titanic3[numeric].groupby("survived").simple.summary()

          resultColumns = ['Column', 'Min', 'Max', 'N', 'NMiss', 'Mean', 'Sum', 'Std', 'StdErr'];

          display(HTML("<h3>Perished</h3>"))
          display(results['ByGroup1.Summary'][resultColumns])          # 1

          display(HTML("<h3>Survived</h3>"))
          display(results['ByGroup2.Summary'][resultColumns])
```

Figure 5. Grouping the Data

Perished

Descriptive Statistics for TITANIC3

	Column	Min	Max	N	NMiss	Mean	Sum	Std	StdErr
survived									
0	pclass	1.00	3.0	809.0	0.0	2.500618	2023.0000	0.744825	0.026187
0	survived	0.00	0.0	809.0	0.0	0.000000	0.0000	0.000000	0.000000
0	age	0.33	74.0	619.0	190.0	30.545363	18907.5800	13.922550	0.559595
0	sibsp	0.00	8.0	809.0	0.0	0.521632	422.0000	1.210449	0.042557
0	parch	0.00	9.0	809.0	0.0	0.328801	266.0000	0.912332	0.032076
0	fare	0.00	263.0	808.0	1.0	23.353831	18869.8951	34.145096	1.201220

Survived

Descriptive Statistics for TITANIC3

	Column	Min	Max	N	NMiss	Mean	Sum	Std	StdErr
survived									
1	pclass	1.00	3.0000	500.0	0.0	1.962000	981.0000	0.872972	0.039040
1	survived	1.00	1.0000	500.0	0.0	1.000000	500.0000	0.000000	0.000000
1	age	0.17	80.0000	427.0	73.0	28.918244	12348.0900	15.061452	0.728875
1	sibsp	0.00	4.0000	500.0	0.0	0.462000	231.0000	0.685197	0.030643
1	parch	0.00	5.0000	500.0	0.0	0.476000	238.0000	0.776292	0.034717
1	fare	0.00	512.3292	500.0	0.0	49.361184	24680.5918	68.648795	3.070067

Figure 6. Grouped Data

We are able to see the main summary statistics for the passengers on the Titanic. This data is summarized by column, giving us the ability to see things such as the mean value of each variable. Looking at this summary, we can immediately see that the passenger class does matter. There is a notable difference in the class of passenger between those who survived and those who perished.

Next, let's look at what happens when we apply some algorithms to the table to more clearly understand the conclusions. Before we can apply these algorithms, we need to build some sampling into the table and add partitioning, as shown in Figures 7 and 8.

```
In [58]:  s.builtins.loadActionSet("sampling")

          # the sampling.stratified action does not accept the vars parameter,
          # copyVars is used to select the columns to copy to the output table
          if 'vars' in titanic3.params:
              del titanic3.vars

          # temporarily set a groupBy parameter
          with titanic3:
              titanic3.groupBy={"survived"}
              titanic3.sampling.stratified(
                  partInd=True,                              # 1
                  samppct=40,                                # 2
                  seed=1234,
                  output={
                      "casout":{"name":"titanic3part", "replace":True},
                      "copyVars":all
                  }
              )

          titanic3.table.dropTable()                         # 3

          titanic3part = s.CASTable("titanic3part")          # 4
          ci = titanic3part.columnInfo()
          display(ci)

          NOTE: Added action set 'sampling'.
          NOTE: Using SEED=1234 for sampling.
```

Figure 7. Adding Sampling

```
In [59]:  survSummary = titanic3part['survived'].groupby('_partind_').simple.summary()

          resultColumns = ["Column", "N", "NMiss", "Mean", "Sum", "Std", "StdErr"]

          display(survSummary['ByGroupInfo'])
          display(survSummary['ByGroup1.Summary'][resultColumns])
          display(survSummary['ByGroup2.Summary'][resultColumns])
```

ByGroupInfo

	PartInd	_PartInd__f	_key_
0	0.0	0	0
1	1.0	1	1

Descriptive Statistics for TITANIC3PART

	Column	N	NMiss	Mean	Sum	Std	StdErr
PartInd							
0	survived	785.0	0.0	0.382166	300.0	0.486227	0.017354

Descriptive Statistics for TITANIC3PART

	Column	N	NMiss	Mean	Sum	Std	StdErr
PartInd							
1	survived	524.0	0.0	0.381679	200.0	0.486263	0.021242

Figure 8. Adding Partitioning

Now that we have partitioned the data, we are ready to add some analytics into the mix. In this case, we choose to use a decisionTree to determine the best characteristics to posses if you wanted to survive the sinking of the Titanic, as shown in Figure 9.

```
In [60]: s.builtins.loadActionSet("decisionTree")                    # 1

          training = titanic3part.query('0 = _partind_')             # 2

          trainingResults = training.forestTrain(
                  target="survived",
                  inputs=all,
                  nominals=char + ["pclass", "survived"],
                  casOut={"name":"forestModel", "replace":True},
                  seed=1234,
                  binOrder=True,
                  varImp=True
          )

          display(trainingResults)

          NOTE: Added action set 'decisionTree'.
```

§ DTreeVarImpinfo

Forest for TITANIC3PART

	Variable	Importance	Std
0	sex	43.636961	20.875796
1	deck	10.966477	6.054770
2	pclass	9.365861	7.859291
3	home.dest	7.420146	3.124172
4	fare	4.423036	3.636955
5	sibsp	3.093761	1.775985
6	age	3.051349	1.929421
7	parch	2.304506	1.842525
8	embarked	1.364805	2.157820

Figure 9. Applying a decisionTree Action Set

The call to LOADACTIONSET in Figure 9 specifies that a decision tree is used as the algorithm of choice. You can see the results of the training of the tree with the variable importance plot. The plot in Figure 9 shows us that the most important variable that predicts survival is not the class of the passenger, but rather the sex of the passenger.

MATPLOTLIB AND D3

Let's look at how we can now visualize the results from the tree using mpld3. As you recall, mpld3 is the API that enables Python to interact with Matplotlib in order to call D# visualizations. By using mpld3, we can take advantage of the power of SAS to process the analytics and then return the data table back to Python. After the returned data is in Python, it can be visualized by the D3 JavaScript language, which allows for interactive charting.

```
In [63]:  import pandas as pd
          import mpld3

          forestAssess_ROC = s.CASTable("forestAssess_ROC", where="1 = _partind_")
          out2 = forestAssess_ROC.to_frame()

          from mpld3 import plugins

          # Define some CSS to control our custom labels


          fig, ax = plt.subplots(figsize=(8, 8))
          ax.set_xlabel('False Positive Rate')
          ax.set_ylabel('Correct Classification Rate')
          ax.set_title('ROC Curve', size=20)
          ax.grid(True, alpha=0.3)

          points = ax.plot(out2._FPR_, out2._Sensitivity_, 'bo-', color='b',
                           mec='k', ms=10, mew=1, alpha=.6, linewidth=1)
          ax.plot(pd.Series(range(0,11,1))/10,pd.Series(range(0,11,1))/10,'k--',linewidth=1)
          # Get data into lists
          my_xpoints = []
          my_ypoints = []
          for i in points:
              my_xpoints.append(i.get_xdata())
              my_ypoints.append(i.get_ydata())

          import numpy as np

          labels = []
          for (j, k) in zip(np.ndenumerate(my_xpoints), np.ndenumerate(my_ypoints)):
              x = str(j).split(",")
              y = str(k).split(",")
              labels.append("<table><tr><th>"+ax.get_xlabel()+"</th><td>"+x[2].strip(')')+"</td></tr><tr> \
                      <th>"+ax.get_ylabel()+"</th><td>"+y[2].strip(')')+"</td></tr></table>")

          tooltip = plugins.PointHTMLTooltip(points[0], labels,
                                             voffset=10, hoffset=10, css=css)
```

Figure 10. Applying mpld3

```
          plugins.connect(fig, tooltip)

          import json
          #mpld3 hack
          class NumpyEncoder(json.JSONEncoder):
              def default(self, obj):
                  import numpy as np
                  if isinstance(obj, np.ndarray):
                      return obj.tolist()
                  return json.JSONEncoder.default(self, obj)
          from mpld3 import _display
          _display.NumpyEncoder = NumpyEncoder

          mpld3.display()
```

Figure 11. Displaying the Data

8

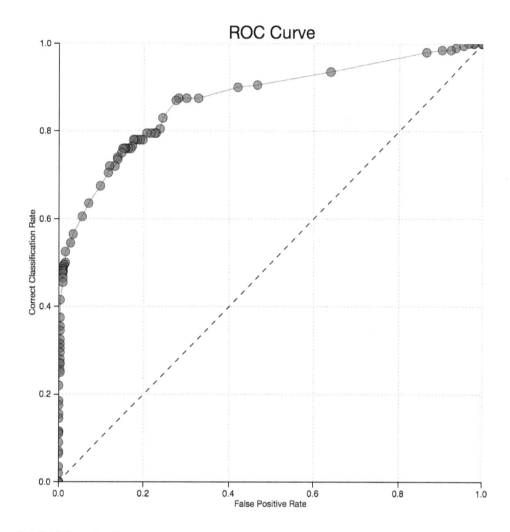

Figure 12. D3 Visualization

12 is a ROC curve chart shown as a D3 visualization. This chart enables you to hover over, click on, and interact with the data that is produced from the code. Not only is the data interactive, but it can be dynamic. By allowing conditional formatting we can use different colors for certain elements of the graph, based on the values of data we retrieve. This feature also allows for dashboarding within a D3 interactive chart.

```python
from mpld3 import plugins

# Define some CSS to control our custom labels

forestAssess = s.CASTable("forestAssess", where="1 = _partind_")
lift = forestAssess.to_frame()

fig, ax = plt.subplots(figsize=(8, 8))
ax.set_xlabel('Percentile')
ax.set_ylabel('Lift')
ax.set_title('Lift Chart', size=20)
ax.grid(True, alpha=0.3)

points = ax.plot(lift._Depth_, lift._Lift_, 'bo-', color='0.5',
                 mec='k', ms=10, mew=1, alpha=.6, linewidth=1)

# Get data into lists
my_xpoints = []
my_ypoints = []
for i in points:
    my_xpoints.append(i.get_xdata())
    my_ypoints.append(i.get_ydata())

import numpy as np

labels = []
for (j, k) in zip(np.ndenumerate(my_xpoints), np.ndenumerate(my_ypoints)):
    x = str(j).split(",")
    y = str(k).split(",")
    labels.append("<table><tr><th>"+ax.get_xlabel()+"</th><td>"+x[2].strip(')')+"</td></tr><tr> \
                   <th>"+ax.get_ylabel()+"</th><td>"+y[2].strip(')')+"</td></tr></table>")

tooltip = plugins.PointHTMLTooltip(points[0], labels,
                                   voffset=10, hoffset=10, css=css)

plugins.connect(fig, tooltip)
```

Figure 13. Applying Conditional Formatting

```python
import json
#mpld3 hack
class NumpyEncoder(json.JSONEncoder):
    def default(self, obj):
        import numpy as np
        if isinstance(obj, np.ndarray):
            return obj.tolist()
        return json.JSONEncoder.default(self, obj)
from mpld3 import _display
_display.NumpyEncoder = NumpyEncoder

mpld3.display()
```

Figure 14. Displaying the Conditionally Formatted Chart

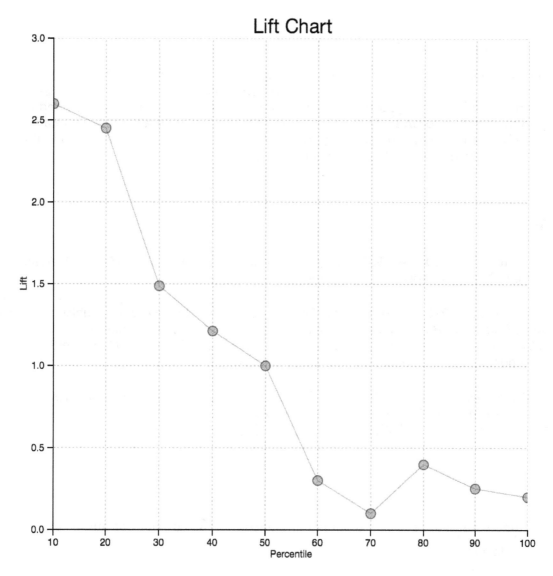

Figure 15. D3 Visualization of Conditionally Formatted Data

Figure 15 is a lift chart shown as a D3 visualization.

CONCLUSION

The ability to include popular JavaScript charting techniques into SAS gives us new options for building interactive charting inside of Python, while harnessing the power of SAS algorithms. The mpld3 project gives us the capability of joining D3 to Python, and SWAT allows Python to talk to SAS. These techniques allow us to build a system that can dynamically produce charting capability, giving open-source users the ability to build amazing interactive charting that is powered by SAS.

REFERENCES

SAS Institute Inc. 2019. SAS Software / python-swat. Accessed April 10, 2019. Available: https://github.com/sassoftware/python-swat.

SAS Institute Inc. 2018. "Programming Considerations for Data-Driven Visualizations." In *SAS Visual Analytics 8.2: Reference.* Cary, NC: SAS Institute Inc. Available https://documentation.sas.com/?cdcId=vacdc&cdcVersion=8.2&docsetId=varef&docsetTarget=n109mqtyl6quiun1mwfgtcn2s68b.htm&locale=en

SAS Institute Inc. 2018. "API Reference." In *SAS Scripting Wrapper for Analytics Transfer.* Cary NC; SAS Institute Inc. Accessed April 10, 2019. Available: https://developer.sas.com/apis/swat/python/v1.4.0/api.html

CONTACT INFORMATION

Your comments and questions are valued and encouraged. Contact the author at:

Joe Indelicato
SAS Institute Inc.
713-325-9857
joseph.indelicato@sas.com

Paper SAS1732-2018

Leverage custom geographical polygons in SAS® Visual Analytics

Falko Schulz, SAS Institute Inc., Brisbane, Australia

ABSTRACT

Discover how you can explore geographical maps using your own custom map regions. SAS® Visual Analytics supports several predefined geo codes including various country and sub-division lookups. However often you have your own custom polygons or shape files drawing exact boundaries of the regional overlay you are trying to explore. From generic sales regions, floor plans or even pipe lines - there are many use cases for custom polygons in visual data analysis. Using custom regions is now easier than ever with a user-interface driven support for importing and registering these custom providers. This paper demonstrates not only the different types of custom providers supported but also shows how to leverage custom polygons within SAS® Visual Analytics by showcasing various industry examples.

INTRODUCTION

Location Analytics is becoming more and more important in today's world of data visualization with business data often associated with location information. A location represents an association to customer address, a store location or sales territory. Data can be stored as single point or a series representing waypoints of a route. Furthermore, locations may represent a specific area such as a state or country. Many organizations may also have their own regions defined from public known fire district or police zones to internal sales regions. Being able to visualize and explore such geographical regions in SAS Visual Analytics is central factor for every data exploration and reporting effort.

ABOUT LOCATION ANALYTICS

SAS Visual Analytics provides a robust and powerful platform to achieve location intelligence performed with a combination of GIS mapping technologies like Esri and SAS Analytics. It enables the creation and distribution of dashboards, reports and allows highly interactive exploration of business visualizations. A range of geo-mapping capabilities provides rich geo visualization from plain reference maps, street maps to high resolution satellite imagery. Customers may also choose to deploy their own GIS server for any special mapping requirements.

With more and more organizations understanding the importance of geo-tagged data, being able to combine business data such as events, weather conditions, social-demographics and more is important to make relevant and informed decisions.

MAPPING TECHNOLOGIES

SAS Visual Analytics leverages various mapping technologies to render geographical maps. By default, the environment provides access to maps provided by the OpenStreetMap community as well as public accessible maps from Esri ArcGIS Online. The latter provides a wide range of map styles from light canvas maps, street or terrain maps to high resolution satellite imagery.

An administrator may also choose to configure their own on-premise or cloud deployment of Esri ArcGIS Server which allows the access to any custom or special organizational maps.

Once configured a user can chose an available background map service in the user interface:

Figure 1 - SAS Visual Analytics map selector

SAS Visual Analytics provides various ways of rendering the data on top of a map. From specific data points or point clustering to regional areas. A user has the choice of the following visualization techniques:

- Bubble plot
- Coordinates plot
- Clustered coordinates plot
- Network plot
- Regional visualization

What type visualization to choose depends on the type of data as well as what location details are available. Network plots are great for things like routes, roads or pipelines but coordinate plots are better suited for customer addresses. Regional or thematic maps are best for geographical areas such as a county, state or sales region.

CUSTOM REGIONAL AREAS

So why do you need the ability to define your own custom regional areas? SAS Visual Analytics provides boundaries for predefined and well known-areas such as countries or state/provinces. Data is provided by GfK GeoMarketing GmbH [Gfk] and regularly updated. The user can select of list of pre-defined types:

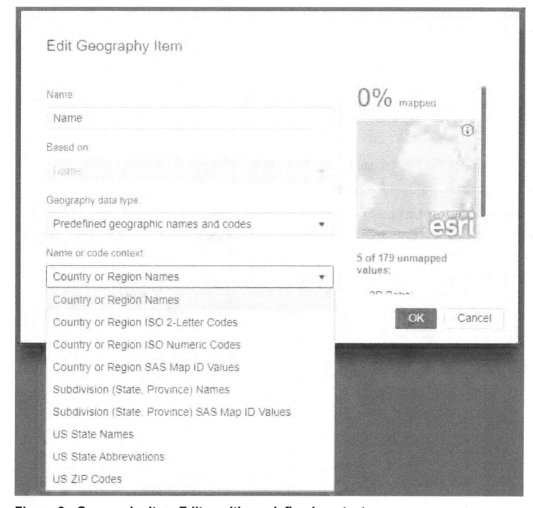

Figure 2 - Geography Item Editor with predefined contexts

For any other regional area or special region, the customer would need to register their own polygon data representing their own custom geographical areas. Examples of custom areas include sales regions, floor plans, property lots, campus maps, districts/zones, etc.

This paper describes the data requirements as well as steps to take for loading such data into SAS Visual Analytics.

Note, the latest version of SAS Visual Analytics 8.2 uses different techniques to load geographical boundaries and as such the steps described for Visual Analytics 7.4 [VA74AdminDoc] are no longer valid.

POLYGON PROVIDER TYPES

SAS Visual Analytics supports two types of polygon providers:

1. SAS Cloud Analytics Services table (CAS Table)
2. Esri ArcGIS Feature Service

If your organization has an existing cloud or on-premise ArcGIS server with feature services containing required polygon data you may choose #2 as your preferred option. An existing feature service doesn't require data import nor any additional storage in the SAS environment and provides quick access to polygon data.

If your polygon data is stored in 3rd party GIS applications or provided in other file formats, you will need to import the data first into SAS Viya.

DATA REQUIREMENTS

Polygon data are usually exported from special GIS applications or CAD systems. As such you may find data in formats such as shape (SHP) or AutoCAD files (DWG/DXF). Regardless of the input format SAS Visual Analytics requires polygon data loaded into CAS and the following structure of the map data set:

Required roles:

- **X/LONG** – represents the x- or longitude coordinate of the data point (Type: *Numeric*)
- **Y/LAT** - represents the y- or latitude coordinate of the data point (Type: *Numeric*)
- **ID** – the unique identifier of the polygon (Type: *Character/Numeric*)
- **SEGMNENT** – if a polygon consists of multiple disconnected areas this column identifies each segment (Type: *Numeric*)
- **SEQUENCE** – a column indicating the correct order of the data points. This column is used for sorting and ensures that correct order is maintained after joining (Type: *Numeric*)

Note, that the names used above are just examples and can be defined by the customer.

	X	Y	id	SEGMENT	sequence
1	-117.5525666	34.072260088	1	1	1
2	-117.5525883	34.072262732	1	1	2
3	-117.5525706	34.072364936	1	1	3
4	-117.5526555	34.072375237	1	1	4
5	-117.5526735	34.072377806	1	1	5
6	-117.5526283	34.072636648	1	1	6
7	-117.5525933	34.072643617	1	1	7
8	-117.5525005	34.072631576	1	1	8
9	-117.5525528	34.072333112	1	1	9
10	-117.5525666	34.072260088	1	1	10
11	-117.5501799	34.072434309	2	1	11
12	-117.5501945	34.072424196	2	1	12
13	-117.5502959	34.072437894	2	1	13
14	-117.5502382	34.072730165	2	1	14
15	-117.5501268	34.072714501	2	1	15
16	-117.5501407	34.072638593	2	1	16
17	-117.5501799	34.072434309	2	1	17
18	-117.5531943	34.074004649	3	1	18
19	-117.5529706	34.075175386	3	1	19
20	-117.5528498	34.075159681	3	1	20
21	-117.5528436	34.075194421	3	1	21

Figure 3 - Example of polygon data set

In order to import polygon data you may choose the provided utility macro `%SHPIMPRT` for importing shape files [Viya33ShapeImport] or select your own method of importing dependent on the data source. You may also utilize the SAS/Graph PROC MAPIMPORT [Graph94MapImport] to import shape files.

Note, regardless of the import method selected – all final polygon data sets need to have the columns outlined before especially the **SEQUENCE** column. To create a sequence variable to enable the polygon segments to be read in the correct order you can use a SAS DATA step and reference the _n_ automatic variable. For example, the following DATA step creates a sequence variable for the MYMAP data set:

```
data mymap;
   set mymap;
   sequence = _n_;
run;
```

Optional you may want to consider reducing the polygon data set size by reducing the density of data points required to render each polygon. Subset your polygon data to decrease the level of detail and improve performance. Reducing the level of detail might also enable you to display a greater number of map regions at one time.

If you have a license for SAS/GRAPH, then you can use the GREDUCE procedure to create a DENSITY variable that enables you to reduce the density of your polygon data. Depending on the source of your map data sets, a DENSITY variable might already be present.

You can use the DENSITY variable in a WHERE statement in a DATA step to reduce the detail in your polygon data. For example, the following DATA step reduces the MYMAP data set to exclude segments that are density level 4 or greater:

```
data mymap;
   set mymap;
   where(density<4);
run;
```

Note: By default, SAS Visual Analytics can retrieve up to 250,000 polygon vertices at a time. If you encounter an error message in a geo map object about the number of polygon vertices, then you might need to reduce the density of your polygon data or filter the data query for your geo map object. In some cases, a very wide ID column in your polygon data can further limit the number of polygon vertices that are retrieved. Check the width of your ID column in SAS Data Explorer if you encounter this message.

If you have data in other formats, e.g. AutoCAD you will need to convert the given file into a shape file using GIS software. Applications such as the open-source QGIS or Esri's ArcMap are very popular and powerful tools. The screenshot below shows the import of an AutoCAD .DWG file into ArcMap and related export dialog to save data into a shape file.

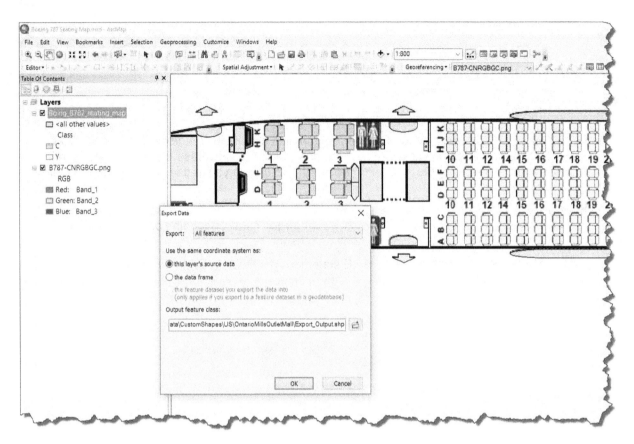

Figure 4 - Esri ArcMap - Export to Shape File

You may also use GIS applications to adjust the projection used in the data. The most common way to reference data points is using unprojected data (latitude/longitude) which also represents the easiest way to register the data later. Users who are not familiar with coordinates spaces and related projections may find it difficult to use your polygon data otherwise.

REGISTRATION

To utilize custom polygonal shapes an administrator will need to register each polygon data source as provider. SAS Visual Analytics 8.2 provides an interface for registration which is accessible from within the geographical item editor. If you select **Custom polygonal shapes** as the geography data type, a list of existing providers is shown.

An administrator can manage and add new polygon providers. An organization may nominate other users for maintaining polygon providers if required. The administrator guide contains details how to setup required permission and group membership.

Given required permissions, registering a new provider is done by nominating a unique name and a user-friendly label. Dependent on the type of the provider (CAS Table vs Esri Feature Service) – you will either need to reference a table or enter the URL of the Esri feature service. The CAS table provider requires additional column mappings and specifying the projection used in the data with the default being WGS84.

The following table shows examples for both provider types and selected values. Each provider may be different so make sure to reference values correctly here or geographical maps may not render correctly.

Figure 5 – List of available polygon providers

CAS Table	Esri Feature Service

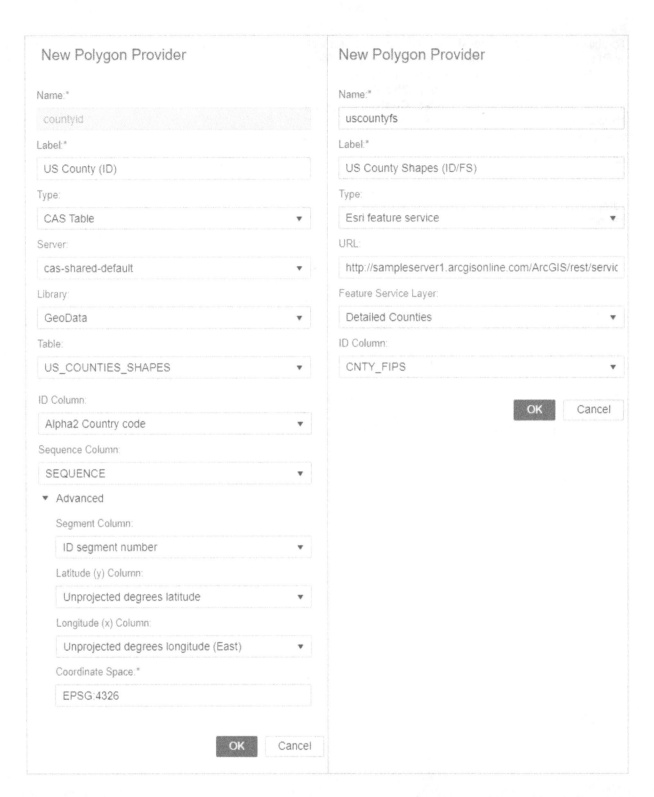

New Polygon Provider

Name:*

countyid

Label:*

US County (ID)

Type:

CAS Table ▼

Server:

cas-shared-default ▼

Library:

GeoData ▼

Table:

US_COUNTIES_SHAPES ▼

ID Column:

Alpha2 Country code ▼

Sequence Column:

SEQUENCE ▼

▼ Advanced

Segment Column:

ID segment number ▼

Latitude (y) Column:

Unprojected degrees latitude ▼

Longitude (x) Column:

Unprojected degrees longitude (East) ▼

Coordinate Space:*

EPSG:4326

OK   Cancel

New Polygon Provider

Name:*

uscountyfs

Label:*

US County Shapes (ID/FS)

Type:

Esri feature service ▼

URL:

http://sampleserver1.arcgisonline.com/ArcGIS/rest/servic

Feature Service Layer:

Detailed Counties ▼

ID Column:

CNTY_FIPS ▼

OK   Cancel

Pay special attention to the **ID** column selected which is required for both types. The value in this column is used as mapping column. Each unique value should match corresponding values in your report data source. The geography item editor will show mapping statistics in the right panel to give you an indication how well a mapping would work:

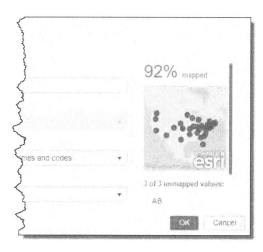

Figure 6 - Geography Item Editor - Mapping Statistics

Note, if you get less than 100% mapped, some data points may be missing during visualization rendering. A related warning sign in the bottom right corner will indicate the missing data.

For more information about registering custom polygon shapes see the VA administration guide [VA82AdminGuide]

USAGE

For a business user, there isn't any additional configuration required to use existing polygon providers. As with any other data item which represents a geographical location the user will need to change the data item classification to be **Geography**. The geography item editor will provide various options to select the correct mapping. As per latest release of Visual Analytics you can select from the following geography data types:

1. Predefined geographic names and codes

2. Custom polygonal shapes

3. Custom coordinates

This paper focuses on type #2 which represent all custom polygon providers which may have been setup before. Select a provider which matches your data source and select the corresponding region ID. Make sure the column selected contains ID values matching the one in the configured provider. A related mapping statistic will give you an indication how well the selected column matches the provider.

VARIOUS MAPPING EXAMPLES

1. US COUNTY BOUNDARIES

This example shows how to register a polygon provider representing the shapes of the United States counties. For the purpose of the example an existing Esri feature service is used provided by the public accessible Esri ArcGIS online examples. The feature service http://sampleserver1.arcgisonline.com/ArcGIS/rest/services/Demographics/ESRI_Census_USA/MapServ er/4 provides such boundary details with the field **FIPS** (5-digit) being the unique identifier for each polygon. Values in this field represent the combined FIPS code for state (2-digit) and county (3-digit). This means data loaded into Visual Analytics will also need to include such ID for correct lookup.

The example uses a data set containing all postal codes of the United States. You can retrieve a copy of the data set if required [ZIPCODE].

The data set also comes with fields for the state FIPS code and county FIPS code. In order for Visual Analytics to lookup county polygons we need to provide a column containing the exact ID as per provider data source. This means it's required to combine both fields into one 5-digit long data item. The following formula is used for a new calculated field named CNTY_FIPS.

The following table shows a preview of the data available (first two columns) and the data item generated (3rd column):

Figure 7 - Calculated field formula to combine state and county FIPS

Two-digit number (FIPS code) for state...	FIPS county code.	CNTY_FIPS	▤
36	103	36103	
36	103	36103	
72	1	72001	
72	3	72003	
72	5	72005	
72	5	72005	
72	5	72005	
72	93	72093	
72	11	72011	
72	141	72141	
72	13	72013	

Figure 8 - Preview of calculated field CNTY_FIPS

With this new column in place we can change its classification to Geography and create a new custom polygon provider. The following options were selected for this Esri feature service based provider:

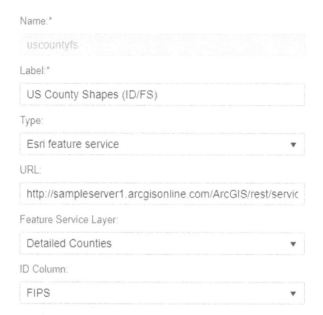

Name:*

uscountyfs

Label:*

US County Shapes (ID/FS)

Type:

Esri feature service ▼

URL:

http://sampleserver1.arcgisonline.com/ArcGIS/rest/servic

Feature Service Layer:

Detailed Counties ▼

ID Column:

FIPS ▼

Figure 9 - Esri feature service provider for US counties

Selecting this provider and using the previous created CNTY_FIPS column as Region ID, provides our new geography data item for US counties. Dropping this data item on the report canvas produces the expected boundaries for the United States counties:

Population density by County

Figure 10 - Example visualization for US county boundaries

2. BUILDING FLOOR PLANS

The following examples shows the boundaries of the San Diego Convention Center [SDCC] including all rooms and levels. The original project was loaded into Esri ArcMap and related boundaries were exported as shape files.

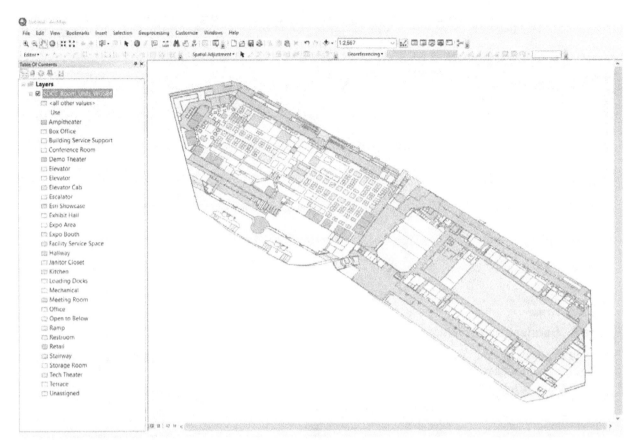

The polygonal data now being available as Esri shape file – we can use the following command to import the data into SAS:

```
proc mapimport datafile="C:\ConferenceFloors\sdcc_floor_plan_wgs84.shp"
      out=work.sdcc_floor_plan;
      id iuid;
run;

proc sql;
      create table mapscstm.sdcc_floor_plan_shapes as
      select x, y, iuid, segment, monotonic() as sequence
      from work.sdcc_floor_plan;
quit;run;
```

Once the data is loaded into CAS, the administrator will be able to configure a new polygon provider referencing this table:

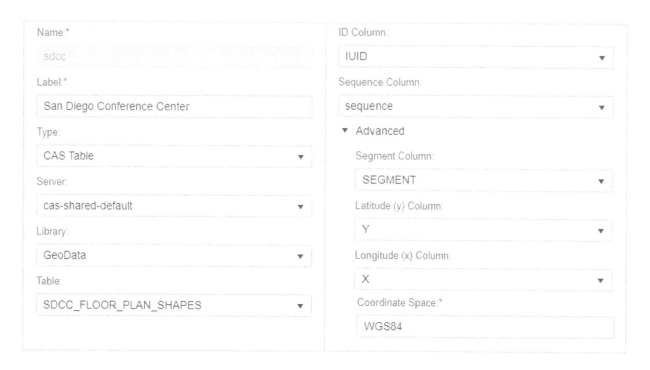

To showcase the usage of boundary data the author created a simple SAS Visual Analytics report allowing the selection of the desired floor, a room search facility as well as usage selection:

Figure 11 - SAS Visual Analytics report showing floor plans for San Diego Convention Center

4. CAMPUS AND AREA MAPS

This example uses data for the buildings of the University of Minnesota [UOM] campus. Similar to the previous example the data has been loaded into Esri's ArcMap first and relevant polygon data have been exported into shape files.

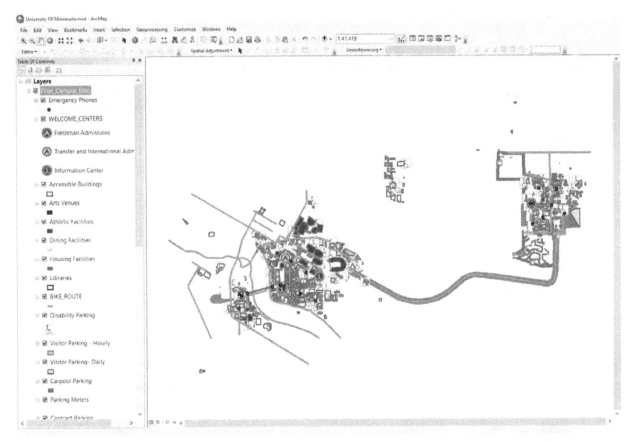

Figure 12 - Esri ArcMap project with polygonal data for campus buildings

A final SAS Visual Analytics report has been created to explore the campus given details available.

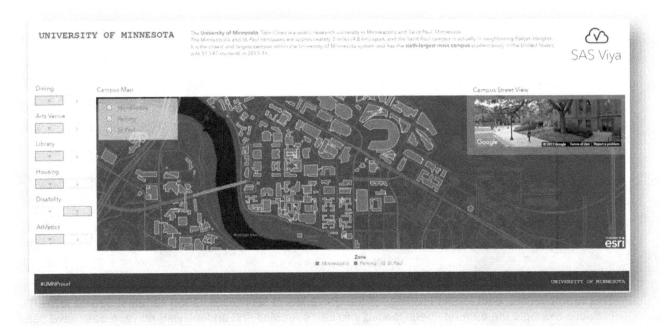

Figure 13 - SAS Visual Analytics report showing the University of Minnesota campus

3. SPECIAL FLOOR PLANS

This is an example using non-standard floor plans. Sometimes you have non-geo referenced floorplans which aren't aligned to any location on earth. As such you can't use a standard background map as you would with any other geo referenced data source.

As example, consider an aircraft seating map with the actual seat being the polygonal shape we are trying to analyze. It may be used by airlines or travel agencies to determine popular seats or simply to lookup seats given a criterion (e.g. exit or seat with disability access).

The data for this example has been prepared using Esri's ArcMap using the built-in editor capabilities. A similar shaped aircraft has been used as reference and as a result seat boundaries may not reflect a real seating layout.

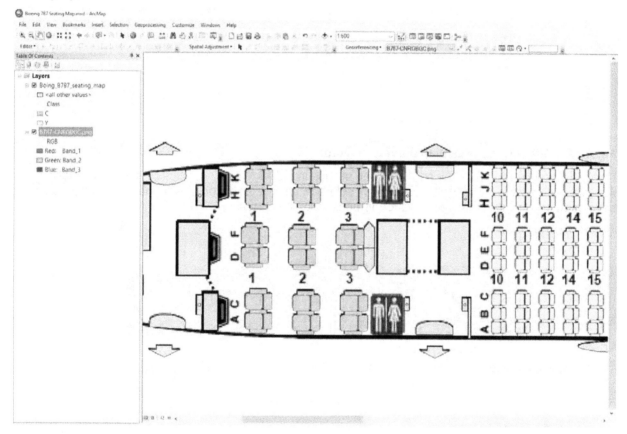

The main difference compared to the previous examples - is that we can't use a standard geographical map background here given the polygons aren't geo referenced. Given that SAS Visual Analytics also supports custom Esri map services the author geo-referenced a custom drawn aircraft image (PNG) and published a new tile-map service.

After polygon provider registration, a new geo map can now reference a custom map service using the service selector:

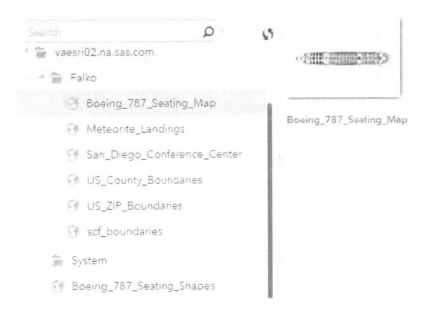

Figure 14 - Visual Analytics map service selector

Using the new polygon provider and new map service in a SAS Visual Analytics report allows analysis of the seats and built-in interactivity allows quick selection using filter options. Note the data for this report have been created using random data for demonstration purposes.

Figure 15 - Visual Analytics report showing aircraft seating map

4. STORE AND TRAFFIC ANALYSIS

The last example shows the building layout of an outlet mall [Ontario] in combination with a special polygon layer showing customer route density. Such layers can be generated using Esri ArcMap and may add additional detail to the geographical area selected for analysis. In the example of the Ontario Mills outlet mall data has been generated to showcase this.

Similar to the example before data has been prepared in ArcMap but this time two of the polygonal layers have been exported to shape files. One representing the building shapes and one the customer route hotspots:

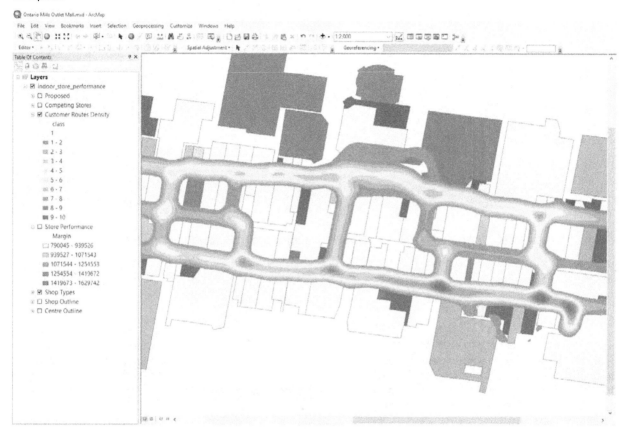

Figure 16 - Esri ArcMap project for outlet map building shapes and customer routes

With custom providers registered and two geo maps created using these providers – the following SAS Visual Analytics sample reports shows how retail store performance analysis could look like in such scenario:

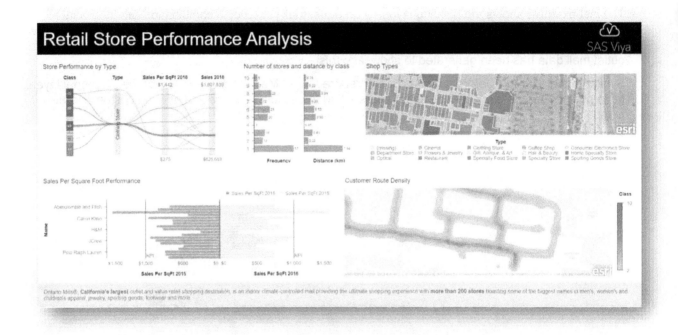

Figure 17 - SAS Visual Analytics report showing retail store performance analysis

CONCLUSION

The ability to import any form of shapes or boundary data into SAS Visual Analytics is a powerful feature. Not only can customers now analyze and visualize non-standard geographical areas but they can also fully understand complex business scenarios and make better decisions based on accurate information. With the support for any type of shape data, from county or province boundaries to complex floor plans, SAS Visual Analytics 8.2 can now be used for advanced location analytics.

With the combination of built-in support for location analysis tools such as clustering, drive-time/live-traffic selection and more – SAS visual Analytics adds valuable insights into your geo-tagged data and creates real value for organizations.

REFERENCES

Schulz, Falko. "More Than a Map: Location Intelligence with SAS® Visual Analytics". August 19, 2014. http://support.sas.com/resources/papers/proceedings14/SAS021-2014.pdf .

[GfK] The map data sets in library MAPSGFK are based on the digital, vector-based maps from GfK GeoMarketing GmbH and are covered by their copyright. http://support.sas.com/mapsonline/gfklicense .

[VA74AdminDoc] SAS Visual Analytics 7.4 Administration Guide, Adding Custom Polygon Data for Geographic Maps, November 2nd 2017, https://support.sas.com/documentation/cdl/en/vaag/69958/HTML/default/viewer.htm#n0g5kjtnbvsrwbn1lxl2wahyc5du.htm

[Graph94MapImport] SAS 9.4 Programming, SAS/GRAPH: Mapping Reference, MAPIMPORT Procedure

http://go.documentation.sas.com/?cdcId=pgmmvacdc&cdcVersion=9.4&docsetId=grmapref&docsetTarget=p031mmm914jrkwn1e4r5ec19xcvm.htm&locale=en

[Viya33ShapeImport] SAS® Viya™ 3.3 Administration, Loading Geographic Polygon Data as a CAS Table http://go.documentation.sas.com/?docsetId=caldatamgmtcas&docsetTarget=p1dwawsidsczlpn121j0glleic xp.htm&docsetVersion=3.3&locale=en

[VA82AdminGuide] SAS VA Administration, Working with Geography Data Items, Create a Geography Data Item By Using Custom Polygonal Shapes

http://go.documentation.sas.com/?cdcId=vacdc&cdcVersion=8.2&docsetId=vareportdata&docsetTarget=p 031vp9uc5y5iun0zipy3c1trkqn.htm&locale=en#p1a7fw0vj2w6aln18sl77suu45o3

[ZIPCODE] SAS Technical Support, Latest United States zipcode dataset,
http://support.sas.com/rnd/datavisualization/mapsonline/html/misc.html

[SDCC] Esri ArcGIS Map Gallery, SDCC_RoomUnits,
http://www.arcgis.com/home/item.html?id=7890a4576813473f8f0384f26a474c2c, data obtained November 2017

[UOM] Esri ArcGIS Map Gallery, TC_Campus_Map_Layers_ALL,
http://www.arcgis.com/home/item.html?id=84e9c3e04c394e5c972627082d0ef6a8, data obtained November 2017

[Ontario] Esri ArcGIS Map Gallery, OntarioMillsShop,
http://www.arcgis.com/home/item.html?id=bced8dd994f843cea0c7595a13f56a05, data obtained November 2017

ACKNOWLEDGMENTS

I would like to thank Jeff Phillips and Eric Short for their assistance about details on geo analysis and their critical role in improving the Geographical visualization component and associated map algorithms.

RECOMMENDED READING

- *SAS® Viya™ 3.3 Administration*

CONTACT INFORMATION

Your comments and questions are valued and encouraged. Contact the author at:

Falko Schulz
SAS Institute Australia
1 Eagle St
Brisbane, QLD, 4001
Phone: +61 7-3233 320
Falko.Schulz@sas.com
http://au.linkedin.com/in/falkoschulz

SAS3427-2019

A Practical Guide to Responsive Reactive Design Using SAS® Visual Analytics

Elliot Inman, Olivia Wright, and Mark Malek, SAS Institute Inc., Cary, NC

ABSTRACT

While it may seem as if you need to be an artist to create the kinds of beautiful, interesting, interactive visualizations you see on many commercial websites, you don't. All you need is a basic understanding of how HTML5 works and how human beings process visual information. In this paper, we provide guidelines for using SAS® Visual Analytics to create websites that are responsive and reactive. Responsive design relies on HTML5 technologies to dynamically adjust HTML content to the screen size and orientation of a web-connected device. This enables websites to work well on many different devices, but it can cause problems. We present guidelines that reduce trial-and-error testing and describe common responsive design issues (resized legends, squished graphs, and more). We show how to easily test the responsiveness of a report using web developer views built into Google Chrome and Mozilla Firefox, and we provide warnings for some known issues with different browsers. Reactive design focuses on how a website responds to users' interactions, in particular, the speed and sensibility of response to human input. We describe how to implement a reactive design creating a smooth workflow of finger swipes or mouse clicks, how to use white space and negative space to draw users' attention, how to use color in headers and graphs to associate related content, and other tips for enabling users to maintain a mental map of dynamic content, quickly accessing the information they need to know.

INTRODUCTION

SAS Visual Analytics 8.3 uses HTML5 to render reports. For web developers who code in HTML, write CSS, and use frameworks like Bootstrap to develop web-based applications, HTML5 enables development of highly responsive web content. With HTML5, text, pictures, and other content automatically resize and rescale for whatever interface is being used from desktop monitor to smart phone, tablet, and so on.

Data scientists often have a broad skill set of statistical, programming, and subject matter expertise, but they are not necessarily web developers. One advantage of SAS Visual Analytics for data scientists is that they don't have to become web developers to deliver high-quality professional web-based reporting. By following a few simple guidelines, data scientists and other report developers can create web-based reporting that takes advantage of HTML5 functionality. This paper describes how to transition a set of traditional tab-based reports into a responsive scrolling report that will look and respond like modern websites. All of this functionality is standard in SAS Visual Analytics.

In this paper, the use case is child social services data. The data includes nine years of state child services metrics, including the number of children served by state child services, the number of children adopted and still waiting to be adopted, and some data on financial subsidies for adoptive parents. The purpose of these reports is to fulfill data transparency requirements for federal regulations regarding the collection of state-level data on child services. We should note that the authors of this paper have created all the reports in this paper, including both the typical "before" and improved "after" reports.

After a description of the data, we show how to modernize a set of traditional reports, including guidelines for focus, flow, standardization, and simplification of disjoint content into a single, flowing responsive report. We describe how users can go beyond the basics and experiment with more unusual ways of creating reactive reporting. We then discuss some of the challenges of working with HTML5.

THE DATA (U.S. FOSTER CARE AND ADOPTION DATA)

In this paper, the data is public data from the United States Administration on Children and Families (ACF), a division of the United States Department of Health and Human Services. Links to all the raw data are provided in the References section of this paper.

The data includes state-level data for all 50 states, Puerto Rico, and the District of Columbia for children served by state social services programs. The data collection program is called the Adoption and Foster Care Analysis and Reporting System (AFCARS). AFCARS data includes state-level data on children entering and exiting child services, adopted and waiting children, and other metrics. The AFCARS data is available in Excel format here. As of the publication of this paper, the national data set included state-level data from fiscal years 2008 to 2017. For technical definitions of the variables used in these reports, readers can review the technical notes from ACF in their data summary.

In addition to the historical data set made available, ACF makes available data on subsidies provided to prospective adoptive parents to assist in managing the needs of potential adoptees. This is an important source of support for high needs children for whom adoption might carry a significant financial challenge for parents. This subsidy data was extracted from PDF reports and merged by state and year with the AFCARS data. Subsidy data from 2008 to 2016 is available, but no data is available for 2017. When merged with the historical data set from AFCARS, the final data structure excluded all data from 2017. Thus, the final data set included all AFCARS national data set and subsidy data for the years 2008 to 2016.

Two additional variables were calculated: the Adopted/Waiting ratio and the Exiting/Entering ratio. Each metric is the simple ratio of two counts calculated to provide a comparable measure across states that vary significantly in population. The Adopted/Waiting ratio is the ratio of adopted children to children still waiting for adoption in that fiscal year for that state. The ratio can exceed 1.0, suggesting that there were more children adopted than waiting, but the ratio is the number of children adopted that year relative to the number of children *still waiting* for adoption at the end of that year. More children could have entered the system than exited.

The Exiting/Entering ratio was calculated the same way. This ratio is a broader measure of all children served by that state's child services division, including those children temporarily removed from a home, reunited with family or other relatives, and otherwise served by various programs for children in the state's care. Again, this ratio can exceed 1.0 for the same reason previously described.

For SAS Visual Analytics reporting, the wide data structure with years and variables repeated in columns was transformed into a tall data structure with years and variables in rows. In the following examples, we show data for several specific states. These states were not chosen for any particular reason.

MODERNIZING TRADITIONAL REPORTING

Figure 1 is a typical example of tab-based reporting. There are five tabs of reports; three tabs are shown.

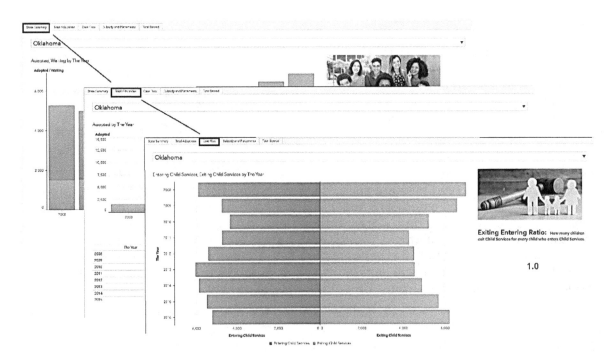

Figure 1. Traditional Reporting

There is nothing fundamentally wrong with this structure. It works. Users know to skip from tab to tab to view individual reports, each of which has a descriptive unique name. There is some notable redundancy over the reports, including repeated state drop-down selections and duplicate tables, but the reports could be linked to allow for a single state selector that filters all reports and a single data view tab for the data. That could be done to improve the usefulness of these reports. However, if you compare this reporting to many modern websites, you will see two obvious differences.

The first difference is how modern websites capture *focus* with the shape and positioning of the content. Most desktop monitors are no longer square in shape; they are rectangular. But many modern websites don't actually fill that rectangular space from left to right. Substantial empty "white space" margins draw the content into the center. This is, in fact, exactly where most users are looking. Users do not read a rectangular monitor as they once read a printed book or newspaper starting top left and working down. For many data scientists, thinking about the shape of reporting might seem strange, but after you compare your reporting to popular modern websites, you realize how much web-based reporting has changed.

The second difference is the *flow* of the content. In the early days of software development when the computer mouse was first being used in conjunction with a keyboard, software developers were cautioned to minimize the number of physical leaps required to jump from two-hands typing to one hand on a mouse. Only the most poorly designed interface would require a user to constantly switch back and forth. In the modern age, the equivalent advice might be to minimize the number of times a user has to click versus scroll using a mouse. Modern websites flow downward with additional content becoming available via a scrolling mouse or, in the case of a smart phone, a swipe of the finger or thumb.

Figure 2 shows a set of tab-based reports on the left and the single scrolling report on the right. Each of the tab-based reports requires a state selection at the top. There is duplication of one type of graph for two different purposes. A waterfall plot is used for Children Adopted and, on another tab, for Children Served. Following tab order, the reports seem to bounce from a more detailed metric (Percent Subsidized) to a more general one (Children Served). And some information is redundant, for example, the first tab includes Children Adopted and Children Waiting in the stacked bar chart, but the first waterfall plot shows Children Adopted.

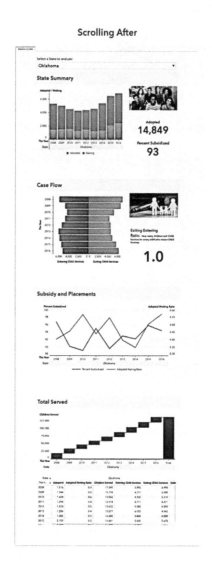

Figure 2. Before and After Reporting

Figure 3 shows some of the major changes made in restructuring the reporting into a more responsive, reactive design.

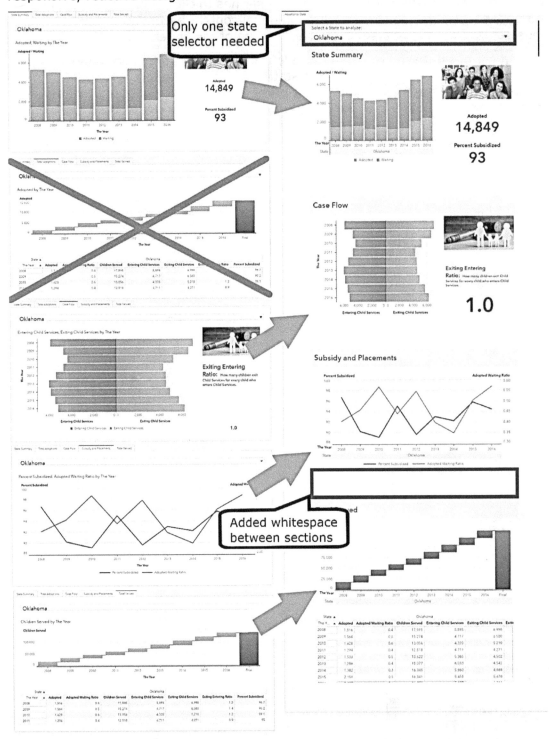

Figure 3. Major Design Changes

The following guidelines describe the steps to create the report in SAS Visual Analytics.

OPTIMIZE FOCUS AND FLOW

Guideline	Implementation in SAS Visual Analytics 8.3 (and later)
Enable Scrolling	Create a new blank tab. In Report > Options > Layout, uncheck the **Avoid Scroll Bars** check box. This one step will enable you to stack one report on top of another into a scrolling structure.
Create Graphic Organizers	In the scrolling report, users no longer have the benefit of tab titles. For each tab in the old report, create a heading in the new report. For ours, we have used text boxes with a gray background and a relatively large 22pt font. Use the same consistent size and style for each "page break" in your scrolling report. Note how "State Summary," "Case Flow," "Subsidy and Placements," and so on provide a dynamic type of section break.
Build Margins	Create margins by adding empty text boxes. For the text box, under Options > Layout > Width, we used 15% for the specified width. Select the **Extend width if available** and **Shrink width if necessary** options to allow HTML5 to dynamically adjust the sizing. The new report now draws the user's focus to the center of the screen with white space margins on the side.
Increase Whitespace	Add empty text boxes to separate content. For these reports, under Options > Layout, we used 10% height. The width of the text box was set to 70%, which is the width minus the margins. When scrolling through the report, users need some type of visual cue of a transition. The gray headers and white space between visualizations help distinguish the topic for each visualization.
Order the Reporting	On the left side of the SAS Visual Analytics report development window, there are three icons: Data, Objects, and Outline. The Outline View enables you to insert the previously developed tab-based objects in the new desired order by dragging and dropping them into the new page.
Maximize the View	Although the tab reporting structure is gone, you want users to be able to view each visualization in the greatest possible detail all at once, filling the monitor screen even as they scroll. Most of the visualizations here have a height set at 70%, leaving some room for the header and white space separating reports. The height specification ensures that the rendering of the report will make enough room for the visualization, regardless of the screen.

Table 1. Guidelines for Focus and Flow

The previous steps will transform a set of tab-based reports into a single flowing scrollable report. However, simply combining the individual reports can create some expected problems: repeated selections, content that appears out-of-place, and report design inconsistencies that might not have been noticed before. The following guidelines should help to reduce these issues.

STANDARDIZE AND SIMPLIFY

Guideline	Implementation
De-duplicate	Remove duplicate visualizations that convey the same information. The "Total Adoptions" tab is not needed as adoptions are on the previous graph. Remove duplicate prompts if possible. One state selector at the top filters all reports.
Delete Unnecessary Content	Remove any titles and legends that are not necessary. Look at the bottom of the "Children Served" report . The original tab-based report included the graph title "Children Served by the Year," but that title is omitted in the new design. The content of the visualization should be obvious from the X-axis and Y-axis labels and, without that title, there is more room for the data. When rendering the report, browsers will no longer have to make room for that title.
Validate Interactions	Ensure that tab-specific interactions still work and are reasonable for that visualization. A single scrolling report can create a set of complex interactions. For this report, the graphs still provide interactive content, but there is only one main selection at the top of the report for state. That one selector filters all visualizations in the scrolling report.
Leave a Trail	One of the benefits of an initial selection is that the user's choice is immediately active in working memory. The user just made a choice and expects a filtered report. However, users returning to the same report might not realize that the state selection affects all reporting. For that purpose, we have added lattice columns where possible. The "State Summary" and "Subsidy and Placements" sections use the lattice. There will never be more than one state on the lattice, but it is helpful to remind users that the state filter is on.

Guideline	Implementation
Minimize Hidden Information	Suppose a user never interacts with any aspect of the report after making an initial selection. Is all of the information required to understand the visualizations actually available? There is a tendency of some report developers to rely too heavily on hover-overs and other interactive features to present critical information. Hover-over functionality should be used only to answer two questions: What is this entity and what is the value? If additional information is critical for the user, it should be available elsewhere on the report.
Standardize Color	Tab-based reports might have reused colors to represent certain variables or conditions. This should be avoided in any reporting process, but it is easily overlooked, especially with a large number of tab-based reports. In a scrolling report, this problem exacerbates potential confusion. The "Children Served" section was changed to a more unique color to avoid confusion with other greens in the report.
Scaffold General to Specific	Visualizations that summarize trends should appear at the top of the scrolling report. Detailed information like text explanations and data tables should appear at the bottom.

Table 2. Guidelines to Standardize and Simplify

By using the method described, data scientists with little or no formal training in web development or HTML5 coding can create reports that look much more like modern, responsive, reactive websites. However, the shift from a traditional to modern flow and focus is just the start. Data scientists interested in going further can experiment with additional ways of implementing even more unusual reporting.

EXPERIMENTING WITH REACTIVE DESIGNS

Any user would agree that simply tabulating all of the subsidy data for every state every year in a single PDF would result in a very hard-to-digest report. The facts would be accurate and reporting requirements could be fulfilled, but it would be a report not easily understood. Figure 4 shows how some of this data is currently reported.

Of Those Children\Youth Adopted During Each Of The FYs 2012 Through 2016 - Distribution Of Those Receiving An Adoption Subsidy

Figure 4. Data Table as PDF

Figure 5 shows a very traditional report for the same data. The purpose of this report is to enable users to compare subsidy rates for different states over time. This data includes states, so the report designer has used a map. Over to the right, the same Percent Subsidized data on the map is split into years. Below those visualizations is a data table with all of the specific data. All three objects interact. Selecting a state on the map filters the data-by-year bar chart and the data in the table. There is nothing particularly wrong about this report, but neither is it particularly meaningful or appealing.

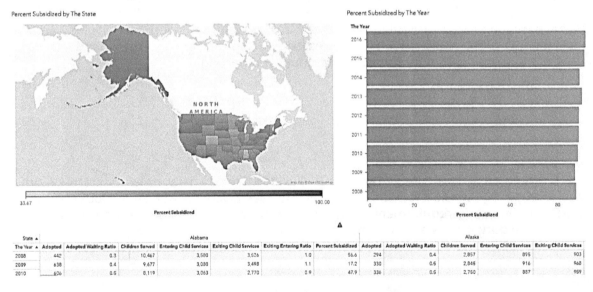

State ▲			Alabama						Alaska			
The Year ▲	Adopted	Adopted Waiting Ratio	Children Served	Entering Child Services	Exiting Child Services	Exiting Entering Ratio	Percent Subsidized	Adopted	Adopted Waiting Ratio	Children Served	Entering Child Services	Exiting Child Services
2008	442	0.3	10,467	3,580	3,526	1.0	56.6	294	0.4	2,857	895	903
2009	638	0.4	9,677	3,080	3,498	1.1	17.2	330	0.5	2,846	916	960
2010	606	0.5	8,119	3,063	2,770	0.9	47.9	336	0.5	2,750	887	959

Figure 5. Traditional Report: Map, Bar Chart, Data Table

The first weakness is the map. The geographic location of states in the United States prominently features Alaska, minimizes Hawaii, and, in the case of this data, does not show the District of Columbia or Puerto Rico at all. The map does nothing to improve our understanding of this data. Different states have different policies that do affect outcomes for at-risk youth, but there is nothing about longitude and latitude or geographic proximity that has any meaning here. In fact, the reason we are using *rates* of subsided adoption is because *counts* of subsidized children would show California, Texas, and Florida different from other states based only on population size. Counts would be misleading in the same way that the sheer square area of land is not meaningful. The map is convenient and perhaps even expected, but it is not very useful and might actually distort the meaning of the metric.

The second weakness is the fact that the additional data is presented at both too high and too low a level to be easily understood. The bar chart provides the data for all states combined or one state at a time, but the chart provides no opportunity to compare states over time. Conversely, the data table provides so much detailed information that it would be difficult to glean any insight from it. Years are in rows, but states are in columns, which makes comparisons impossible.

Beyond those problems, the subdued green coloring does little to interest any user. You could argue that color choice reflects the seriousness of the topic, but the subdued color does not catch the attention of a viewer. Again, the report is not wrong, just not very helpful and definitely not very interesting.

Figure 6 is a radically different version of the same report. This report uses a time slider at the top to allow users to select any period of time between 2008 and 2016. Despite the fact that the bars below the time slider are purple and not a black-and-white ASCIImatic, they are indeed a box plot. And below that is a word cloud with the data in row order. In the same amount of space and using the same data as the traditional report, we have a completely different design.

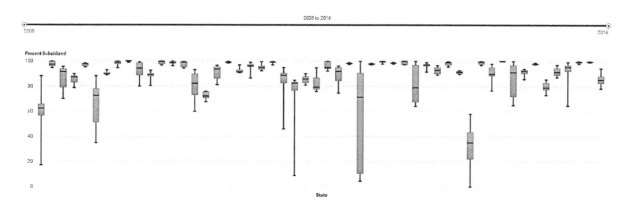

Figure 6. Reactive Report

The map is gone, as are the state name tick marks on the box plot. In the word cloud, size and color were both mapped to the Percent Subsidized variable such that a larger state name in green indicates a higher percent of subsidized adoptions. No formal training is needed to understand this report as it is completely interactive.

As Figure 7 shows, selecting a bar selects the state and provides the box plot data associated with it.

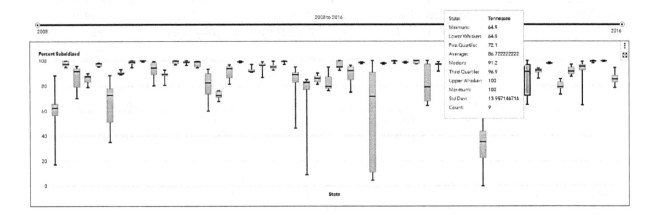

Tennessee

Figure 7. Top Down: Selecting a Bar

Figure 8 shows how selecting a state from the word cloud below selects the state in the box plot.

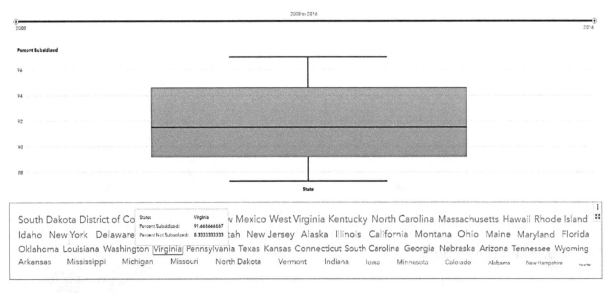

Figure 8. Bottom Up: Selecting a State

While this report occupies a single screen, a few additional aesthetic changes can make the report even better. For example, by adding a background color to the time slider and a color border around the box plot and word cloud, it becomes absolutely clear that the three objects are related. In the case of the time slider, the background color is a significant improvement and keeps that single straight line from becoming lost at the top of the screen.

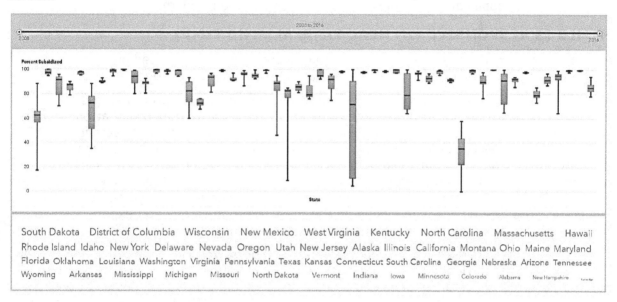

Figure 9. A Color Coordinated Report

While creating a report like this cannot be summarized in a set of next-do-this steps, there are a few guiding principles that can assist in inspiring your experimentation.

Suggestion	Implementation
Eschew the Mundane	Do not repeat visualizations out of mere convenience or habit. The data in these reports is state-level data easily mapped, but there is virtually nothing about the geospatial location of the data that has an effect on the outcomes for foster care children. Why map the data?
Delete, Delete, Delete	Experiment with a stripped-down version of visualizations that do not include titles or axis labels. The states are not listed on the X axis in this visualization, but when you select a bar, you see the state in the hover-over and in the word cloud below.
Misuse the Software	In SAS Visual Analytics, we distinguish "Graphs" from "Controls," but interactivity means that most graphs can be used as a control. Instead of being used to demonstrate a finding, a word cloud can be used as a control.

Table 3. Suggestions for Experimentation

SAS Visual Analytics reporting using HTML5 provides a modern platform for data visualization. But the responsive nature of HTML5 and the deployment of reporting on many different shapes and sizes of screens can create some problems.

HTML5 IS RESPONSIVE (IN REAL TIME, ALL THE TIME)

HTML5 will automatically adjust any SAS Visual Analytics reporting based on screen size, user input, and certain aspects of the report, as it tries to fit content onto a screen.

The rise in popularity of rectangular screens for desktop computers prompted the development of web-reporting with wide white space margins to draw users' attention back to the center of the screen. Report developers should, for now, assume a rectangular horizontal screen as the default desktop view. But there are large number of significantly different-sized screens: jumbo wide view screens in conference rooms, tiny smart phone screens held vertically, and a large array of differently proportioned tablet screens. Suffice to say, HTML5 will attempt to adjust reporting to fit those screens, and some aberrations will occur. The best advice is to design on the most common screen you expect users to have and follow the previous guidelines to avoid some pitfalls.

Using the Chrome browser, if you select **Developer Tools**, you will have the option to view whatever web page is loaded in the browser dimensions you choose, as well as on many common devices like smart phones and tablets. This should give you a chance to see how reports under development will respond when rendered with HTML5.

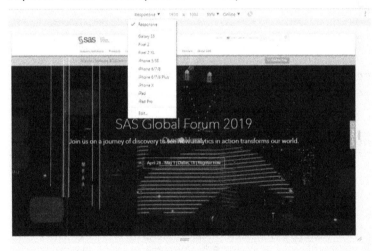

Figure 10. Chrome Emulation of Various Screen Dimensions

In adjusting for screen size, SAS Visual Analytics attempts to preserve as much meaningful content as possible, but certain content is often lost. Legends for graphs are often abandoned. Pie charts in particular, which have issues of interpretability due to misreading of slice sizes, require significant additional context (titles, callouts, legends) and a lot of additional space around the chart. Figure 11 illustrates the same pie chart rendered in increasingly smaller size and the problems that result. Following the previous guidelines to reduce unnecessary titling and text will help to keep the visualization front-and-center on any screen. Nevertheless, some visualizations like pie charts should be used sparingly.

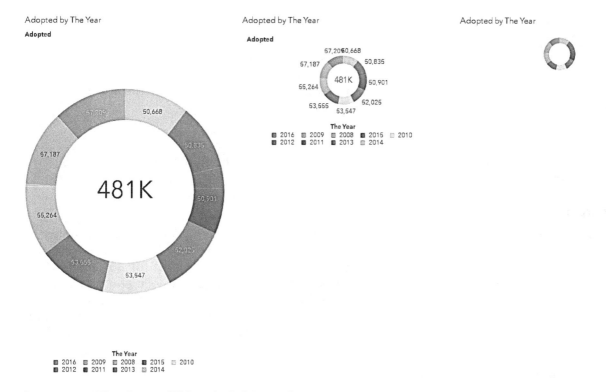

Figure 11. The Incredible Shrinking Pie

NOT ALL BROWSERS ARE ALIKE

One of the first major advances in desktop publishing was the advent of WYSIWIG word processing software in the late 1970s, commercialized in the 1980s. WYSIWIG – what you see is what you get – meant that documents would print exactly as they looked on the screen. HTML5 is definitely not WYSIWIG.

With the rise of the internet, HTML ("hypertext markup language") provided a common standard for web-based page layout, but dynamic content often rendered inconsistently. The Java Runtime Engine offered the promise of write-once-run-anywhere and provided a common engine for internet multimedia. Later, Adobe Flash/Flex provided an even more adventurous, yet safe space for dynamic visualizations, video, and sound. The current rise of HTML5 offers much of the same promise of these past technologies: HTML5 tags will be processed the same by different browsers and the rendered content will be presented as intended to users. Of course, this is not always true. What you expect to see is not always what appears on the screen.

If your organization has standardized to a particular browser (for example, all desktops have Chrome) and you know users will use that browser, develop and test using Chrome. The same for Firefox, Edge, Safari, and others. The problem is more complex if you are serving content such as public reporting where end users can use whatever they prefer, and this does not begin to account for tablets and mobile devices. The best way to assess browser usage is to audit weblogs of access to your reports, but that often requires more advanced web analytics and IT skills. Report developers who want a quick estimate of the most HTML5 compliant browsers should check HTML5TEST. SAS regularly publishes the results of our own browser testing at support.sas.com.

OTHER CONSIDERATIONS

The majority of this paper has focused on modernizing reporting with very little attention to two issues of importance: usefulness and appropriateness. Those are important questions worth considering. First, do all of the changes suggested here actually make the reporting more useful? Second, are there some situations in which this type of modern reporting is simply not appropriate?

USEFULNESS

Current federal law requires these data to be collected. Gathering the data does involve costs to states to collect, validate, and submit these metrics. Whether that effort is worth the cost is often under reconsideration, as noted in this 2018 notice to the Federal Register regarding the AFCARS data.

As data scientists, we believe in the importance of gathering, analyzing, and communicating findings from data. Analyzing AFCARS data advances our understanding of how best to meet the needs of at-risk children receiving state social services. But to fulfill the goals of data science, we must report the data in a manner that the general public and researchers can use it. That means the data will be available on the internet. That means that reporting must allow users to interact with the data, not just read a PDF or download a file. Users must be able to ask questions and interrogate the data. A *useful* reporting design allows users to do so.

Why, then, do we need to implement a modern, responsive, reactive design? Because users expect it. Users expect that the data will be supported by reporting that makes the data seem relevant and important to people today.

A modern reporting design reinforces the current present usefulness of the data. As new technologies are developed, we regularly transition old content to new formats. Printed books are scanned; paintings are photographed with digital cameras; and vinyl records are transformed into digital sound. But not all content is carried forward. Not all books or paintings or music are transformed to be a part of our modern digital world. In truth, we import into the future only what we value from the past.

The AFCARS data has always been an important source of information about state efforts to serve at-risk children and find permanent homes for children without them. Modernizing such reporting makes clear that this data and the issue, itself, are still important to us. Simply stated, making these reports more modern will make the data more likely to be used and thus, more modern reporting is more useful.

APPROPRIATENESS

The reporting here is based on anonymized aggregated data at the state level, but the data represent the lives of millions of American children, including those who have been adopted, those waiting for adoption, and the hundreds of thousands of children served every year by state child services agencies. The data represents an objective, straightforward accounting of the positive outcomes and continuing risks for millions of young people.

This is a serious story to tell. Is it possible that more traditional reporting like the map-based report with its subdued greens, technical layout, and stuffed-with-facts data table is more "appropriate" than the interactive report in shades of purple and green? That is a challenging question.

In practice, we have seen data scientists and report developers who pursue an aesthetic designed to evoke the seriousness of the subject: black screens filled with rows of gray gauges or a half-a-dozen complex graphs of all sorts squeezed onto a single screen – all designed to create the impression of a tremendous amount of critical information, all of which must be processed at once. There is nothing fundamentally wrong with that, if that is what users expect. There are limitations to human cognitive capacity in terms of working memory and attention and those designs can tax the resources of any human mind. At the same time, experts in any field often want and need much more detailed information than novices. Experts expect complexity.

On the other hand, the most "appropriate" design may be the one least like what has been done in the past. Human beings have an innate desire for novelty. The desire for new experiences drives a large part of human exploration and learning. It is why people want to take a vacation to a place they have never been or read a new book by an unfamiliar author or learn a new programming language or, in fact, design a different kind of report. If, by implementing a more unusual set of reports with brighter colors, more reactive designs, and somewhat unusual ways of presenting the data, we make the data new again, we may inspire others to more deeply consider these data. If our goal is to encourage the careful consideration of these data, such a novel design is "appropriate." The design serves the purpose.

CONCLUSION

This paper presented a set of suggestions for how data scientists and report designers can transform traditional tab-based reporting into more modern, responsive, reactive reporting ready for HTML5 compliant browsers. We described how to take a set of disjointed tab-based reports and integrate them into a single scrolling report that will respond well on a variety of screens. We also made some suggestions for how report designers might take this functionality further, designing very novel visualizations that might inspire users to explore the reporting in greater depth. And we noted some of the challenges posed by auto-adjusting HTML5 and how to anticipate potential problems.

For more information on how to modernize your Visual Analytics reporting, please see Beautiful Reports, a SAS community led by Mark Malek that focuses on visual designs that inspire users. In addition to examples of responsive, reactive scrolling reports, it includes additional content on larger issues such as knowing your audience and ensuring accessibility and technical design content on topics such as formatting text and the use of color.

The AFCARS data used is available as open data. Links to the source data are in the References section of this paper. No matter what the design or technologies used, the ultimate value of reporting rests on the value of the data and issues addressed. The treatment of at-risk youth and efforts to find permanent homes for children in foster care is an issue of enormous importance. The collection and reporting of this data to advance our understanding of these issues is, without a doubt, worthwhile. We hope that, in addition to finding useful guidance on report design, readers will be inspired to think of other ways in which these particular data can be made better known, better understood, and more widely used.

REFERENCES

All links below accessed February 2019.

U.S. Department of Health & Human Services. 2019. https://www.acf.hhs.gov/

"Adoption and Foster Care Analysis and Reporting System," Federal Register, Vol. 83, No. 51. p. 11449. Accessed at https://www.govinfo.gov/content/pkg/FR-2018-03-15/pdf/2018-05042.pdf

"Trends in Foster Care and Adoption." Available https://www.acf.hhs.gov/cb/resource/trends-in-foster-care-and-adoption

"Trends in Foster Care and Adoption (PDF)." Available https://www.acf.hhs.gov/sites/default/files/cb/trends_fostercare_adoption_08thru17.pdf

"AFCARS Data Set with Adoption Variables (Microsoft Excel)." Available https://www.acf.hhs.gov/sites/default/files/cb/afcars_state_data_tables_08thru17.xlsx

U.S. Department of Health & Human Services. 2019. Subsidies data. Available at:

https://www.acf.hhs.gov/sites/default/files/cb/adoption_subsidy2012_2016.pdf

https://www.acf.hhs.gov/sites/default/files/cb/adoption_subsidy_2008.pdf

https://www.acf.hhs.gov/sites/default/files/cb/adoption_subsidy_2009.pdf

https://www.acf.hhs.gov/sites/default/files/cb/adoption_subsidy_2010.pdf

https://www.acf.hhs.gov/sites/default/files/cb/adoption_subsidy_2011.pdf

CONTACT INFORMATION

Your comments and questions are valued and encouraged. Contact the authors at:

Elliot Inman, Ph.D.
Manager, Software Development
SAS Global Hosting and US Professional Services Division
(919) 531-1717
Elliot.Inman@sas.com

Olivia Wright
Software Developer
SAS Global Hosting and US Professional Services Division
(919) 531-3262
Olivia.Wright@sas.com
Twitter: @OliviaJWright
https://www.linkedin.com/in/oliviajwright/

Mark Malek
Visual Designer
SAS Business Intelligence Research and Development
(919) 531-1608
Mark.Malek@sas.com
https://www.sas.com/beautifulreports
https://www.linkedin.com/in/mark-malek-b7a16a8b

Paper SAS3331-2019

Using Custom, User-Defined SAS® Formats with SAS® Visual Analytics on SAS® Viya®

Andrew Fagan SAS Institute Inc.

ABSTRACT

Are formats associated with your data? Formats that you created in SAS® using the FORMAT procedure? If you want to use SAS® Visual Analytics on SAS® Viya® with your data, you need to load your formats so that they can be found. In SAS®9, this meant adding the catalog that contained your formats to the format search path. On SAS Viya, there is an analogous task but the process is different. First, SAS Viya cannot read a SAS catalog, so you need to convert your catalog to a structure that SAS Viya understands. Next, you need to place the formats in a location where SAS Viya can find them. And finally, you need to tell SAS Viya to load the formats whenever a new session is started. This paper explores how you, as a user of SAS Visual Analytics on SAS Viya, can accomplish these steps and make your formats available. You can do this by using SAS® Environment Manager, SAS® Studio, or shell scripts. Each of these methods is described in detail, including sample code, and the benefits and limitations of each are presented.

INTRODUCTION

Formats are commonly used in SAS to map one value to another. Data is often stored as key values or in a shorthand form, but those same values are not always meaningful in a report. One of the simplest examples is date values: SAS stores a date as the number of days since January 1, 1960. It is unlikely many people reading a report would like to see today's date displayed as 21,600 rather than May 1, 2019. So SAS supplies a format that will take as input the number of days and convert it to a number of different friendly date displays.

But SAS can't supply formats for data values that are specific to your data. For that, SAS supplies a procedure (PROC FORMAT) that allows you to create your own formats, mapping one value to another. Many SAS users have made extensive use of this procedure and as a result have a large library of formats associated with their data. In some cases, the data is physically bound to an associated format, so the format must be present in order for the data to be used.

In SAS 9, formats are stored in a catalog and these catalogs can be added to a format search path. The search path is unique to each SAS session, and when SAS encounters data that requests a format, it searches the catalogs in this search path to find it. As long as the format is in a catalog on the search path, SAS can find it and everything works as planned.

SAS Viya can use the same formats used in SAS 9. But making them accessible to SAS Viya is not done in the same way. This paper explains three different options for making your formats accessible to SAS Viya.

THE DATA

The data used in this paper is based on values in the sashelp.cars table that is available with all SAS 9 deployments. The data itself is not an important part of the paper, but it provides several good examples of where you might use formats and for what purpose. Examples of a format on a character field, on a numeric field, formats that map values on-to-one, and formats that are used to categorize values are shown.

Both the data and the formats need to be stored in a permanent location (you cannot use the saswork library). This is because a copy of each will need to be loaded into SAS Viya. For illustrative purposes, the paper assumes they are stored in a directory named C:/temp/SGF2019 on Windows or /tmp/SGF2019 on Linux.

In order to generate the data used, you can submit this DATA step (but don't do it yet, the formats need to be defined first):

```
options fmtsearch=(SGF2019.carFormats) ;

data sgf2019.carData (keep=make model mfgCountry type MSRP msrp_range mpg
mfgAvail) ;
    attrib make length=$13
    model length=$40
    type length=$8
    mfgCountry length=$32 format=$mfgCountry. label="Country of origin"
    mfgAvail length=$32 format=$mfgCurrent. label="Available in US?"
    mpg length=8. format=4.1 label="Combined city/hwy mileage"
    MSRP length=8. format=DOLLAR8. label="Suggested Retail Price in USD"
    msrp_range length=8. format=priceRange. label="Price Range"
    ;
    set sashelp.cars (keep=make model type MSRP mpg_city mpg_highway) ;
    mfgCountry = make ;
    msrp_range = MSRP ;
    mfgAvail = make ;
    mpg = ((.55*mpg_city) + (.45*mpg_highway)) ;
run ;
```

THE FORMATS

The formats associated with the data are simple but illustrate some common usages.

Format name	DB2 Data Type
$mfgCountry.	Maps the manufacturer to the country of origin
$mfgCurrent.	Maps the manufacturer to a simple yes/no on whether it is currently available in the US.
priceRange.	Classifies the price of a vehicle into a category

Table 1. Formats associated with the data used in the paper

These formats are created by using PROC FORMAT and submitting the code to run in SAS.

In order to generate the formats used, you can submit this code:

```
libname sgf2019 "C:\temp\sgf2019" ;
proc format library=sgf2019.carFormats ;
    value $mfgCountry
            "Acura" = "Japan"
            "Audi" = "Germany"
            "BMW" = "Germany"
            "Buick" = "USA"
            "Cadillac" = "USA"
            "Chevrolet" = "USA"
            "Chrysler" = "USA"
            "Dodge" = "USA"
            "Ford" = "USA"
            "GMC" = "USA"
            "Honda" = "Japan"
            "Hyundai" = "Korea"
            "Infiniti" = "Japan"
            "Isuzu" = "Japan"
            "Jaguar" = "United Kingdom"
            "Jeep" = "USA"
            "Kia" = "Korea"
            "Land Rover" = "United Kingdom"
            "Lexus" = "Japan"
            "Lincoln" = "USA"
            "MINI" = "United Kingdom"
            "Mazda" = "Japan"
            "Mercedes-Benz" = "Germany"
            "Mercury" = "USA"
            "Mitsubishi" = "Japan"
            "Nissan" = "Japan"
            "Oldsmobile" = "USA"
            "Pontiac" = "USA"
            "Porsche" = "Germany"
            "Saab" = "Sweden"
            "Saturn" = "USA"
            "Scion" = "Japan"
            "Subaru" = "Japan"
            "Suzuki" = "Japan"
            "Toyota" = "Japan"
            "Volkswagen" = "Germany"
            "Volvo" = "Sweden"
            other = "_unknown_"
    ;

    value $mfgCurrent
            "Isuzu" = "No"
            "Mercury" = "No"
            "Oldsmobile" = "No"
            "Pontiac" = "No"
            "Saab" = "No"
            "Saturn" = "No"
            "Suzuki" = "No"
```

```
              other = "Yes"
     ;

     value priceRange
           0-15000 = "Budget"
           15001-30000 = "Medium"
           30001-40000 = "High"
           other = "Luxury"
     ;
  run ;
```

With both the data and the formats defined, we can try to use them in SAS Viya.

LOADING THE DATA INTO SAS VIYA

There are a number of methods available to load data into SAS Viya. For this example, we will use the Data Import feature available in SAS Environment Manager. The data will be loaded into a library named SGF2019_Data. The exact location of the data is not important to this example: once the formats are defined to SAS Viya, they will be available to any table in any library.

In SAS Environment Manager, choose Data then Import.

Display 1. SAS Environment Manager Data Import

Select Local File and navigate to the location on disk where you saved the carData table.

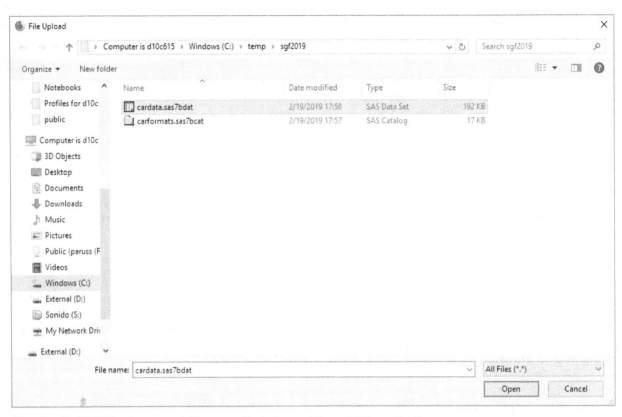

Display 2. SAS Environment Manager Data Import Local File selection

Next, you want to specify the library to load the data into.

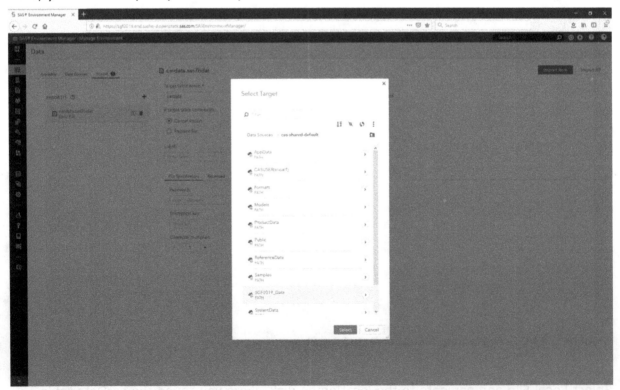

Display 3. SAS Environment Manager Data Import Library selection

The exact library is not important. For this example, I have created a library specifically for the data but it could have just as easily been added to the existing Public library or any other available library that you have the appropriate access to.

Choose Import Item in the top, right corner and your table will be imported.

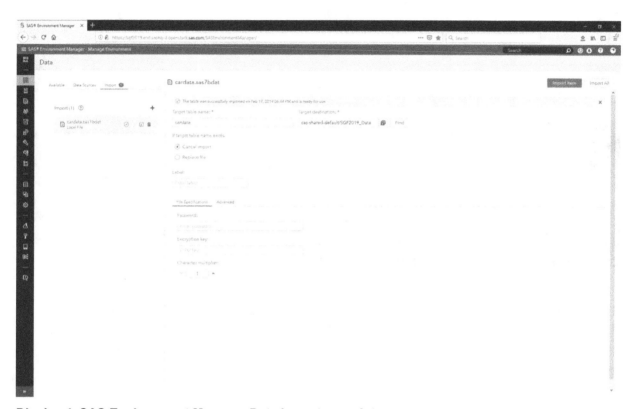

Display 4. SAS Environment Manager Data Import complete

ATTEMPTING TO ACCESS THE DATA WITHOUT THE FORMATS

With the data loaded, you can now try to use the data in SAS Visual Analytics.

In Explore and Visualize Data, choose your carData table to work with.

Display 5. Explore and Visualize Data table selection

Everything looks great until you choose OK. You then get this lovely error message that in its own way is trying to tell you that it can't find the formats associated with your data.

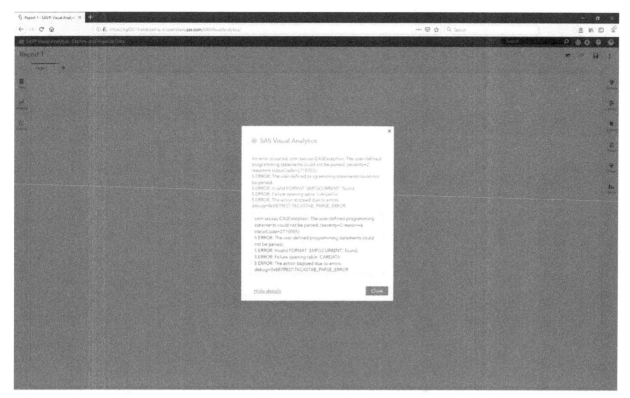

Display 6. Explore and Visualize Data error when opening table

Since the formats cannot be found, the data is inaccessible and any analysis you attempt to perform will fail. There is currently no way to tell SAS Visual Analytics to ignore the formats and proceed (similar to the NOFMTERR option in SAS 9).

Unless you want to go back to your SAS programming environment and re-create the table without referencing any formats, you will need to make the formats available.

METHOD 1: SAS ENVIRONMENT MANAGER

Often the easiest way to make a limited number of formats available to SAS Viya is by using the point and click interface in SAS Environment Manager. This feature is only available to members of the SAS Administrators security group since it impacts the overall configuration for all users.

If you are a member of the SAS Administrators group, you will see a menu option for User-Defined Formats (the very last choice in the System group). The first time you use this feature, the only formats that will be present are those supplied by SAS, stored in a format library aptly named SASSUPPLIEDFORMATS. Once you have added your own formats, they will also be visible on this screen to other administrators as well.

Display 7. Initial User Defined Formats screen in SAS Environment Manager

We need to create a new Format Library where our formats will be stored. This is a special task that requires you to Assume the Superuser role. Click on the corresponding icon at the top left of the screen to temporarily become a Superuser.

Display 8. Assume the superuser role

Once you have assumed the superuser role, the icon representing the creation of a new format library is available. Select it and you can supply the parameters for the new format library. While it is possible to create an empty format library and add formats to it later, we are going to use the shortcut to create the library and populate it with our formats in one step.

The name can be any valid SAS library name. Typically, you want to make this something meaningful, so another administrator will have an idea of what type of formats it contains. The source path field is the OS path to the SAS catalog containing the formats. Note that there is no Browse button for this field, so you must enter it in correctly (cut and paste is your friend). The search order allows you to specify how these formats relate to other format libraries that are already defined. You can choose to put them at the start of the search order, at the end, to replace the existing search order completely, or to add the formats but not put them in the search order at all. Append is typically what you want to do. Be very careful with Prepend or Replace as you will be impacting, and potentially changing in an unforeseen way, existing format usage.

Enter the fields and choose Save.

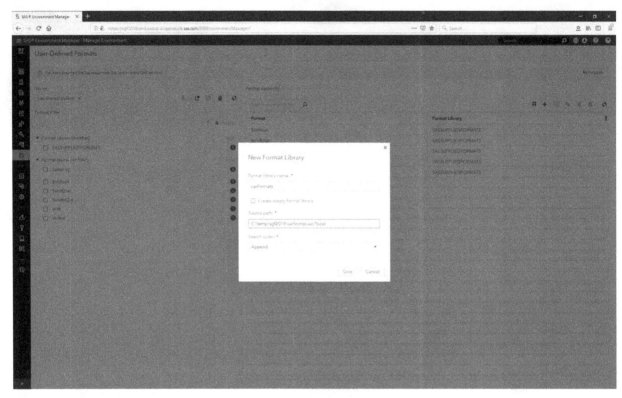

Display 9. Create a new format library

The new format library is created and your formats are added to the search path.

Display 10. New format library created and formats added to the search path

If you return to Explore and Visualize Data, your report will now open successfully.

Display 11. Data available for analysis once the formats are loaded

Success. The formats will remain available to all users until you remove the format library or alter the search path to not include then.

METHOD 2: SAS STUDIO

SAS Environment Manager is an easy way to add a set of formats to your SAS Viya environment. But sometimes the formats change frequently (maybe they are generated based on data values). Or you have a large number of format libraries you want to add. Or maybe you are just one of those people who hates user interfaces. A programmatic approach is often better suited in these cases.

SAS Studio is the programming environment component of SAS Viya. Not only does it provide a familiar looking SAS development environment, but it can communicate with CAS as well. CAS is the underlying server for SAS Viya that needs to have access to the formats. So SAS Studio gives you a single place where you can run the SAS code to create the data and formats, and a programmatic way to make both available to SAS Visual Analytics on SAS Viya.

To invoke SAS Studio, choose Develop SAS Code.

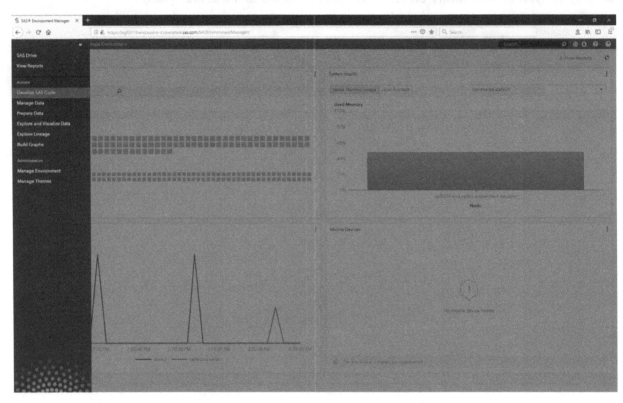

Display 12. Invoke SAS Studio

Initially you get a blank program area. Enter the same code used in the SAS Environment Manager section to create the formats and the data. You can enter the code in or just use cut and paste. Note that the example here is running on Linux rather than Windows. So, the example directory names are slightly different from those used in the SAS Environment Manager section.

Display 13. SAS Studio code to create formats and data

Choose Submit at the top of the program window to have SAS run the code. The log will be displayed, and the formats and data are created.

Display 14. Formats and Data created using SAS Studio

With the data and formats created, we need to make the formats available to SAS Viya. This is done by creating a CAS session in SAS Studio, and then using PROC FORMAT to load the formats into SAS Viya. Note that although I am treating these steps as different programs in order to explain the details, they can all be submitted at the same time as one program.

Back in the SAS Studio program window, submit the following code.

```
/* create a cas session */
cas udfSession sessopts=(caslib=casuser timeout=1800 locale="en_US");

/* assign all the cas libraries */
caslib _all_ assign;

/* Identify format catalogs to move to server */
catname work.mycat(sgf2019.carFormats) ;

/* Collect formats in work.temp */
proc format
    library=work.mycat
    cntlout=temp;
run;

/* Move the format library from SAS Client to Cas session. */
proc format cntlin=temp sessref=udfSession
    casfmtlib='carFormats';
run ;
```

```
/* Promote the format library to global scope */
cas udfSession promotefmtlib fmtlibname=carFormats replace;

/* Save the format library to a table */
cas udfSession savefmtlib fmtlibname=carFormats caslib=Formats
table=carformats replace;
```

Display 15. SAS Studio code to make the formats available

When the code completes, the log will contain information about what was done with the formats.

Display 16. Formats available to SAS Viya after submitting code in SAS Studio

Without a full explanation of what you can do in SAS Studio to interact with CAS, this code does a few things that you should understand.

First, a CAS session is created. This is necessary for any work you want to do with SAS Viya.

Next, all the libraries defined in the SAS Viya environment are mapped to SAS librefs. The one that we are primarily concerned with is the Formats library. This library is predefined for you in every SAS Visual Analytics environment and is used to store a backup copy of any formats that are loaded. This library will have an entry for the sassuppliedformats by default. After we complete the process to make our formats available to SAS Viya, it will also have an entry for carFormats (regardless of whether you use SAS Environment Manager or SAS Studio). The entries in this library are solely for backup purposes in the event the server goes down. They are not used during regular SAS Viya usage and can be deleted at any time if it is determined there is no need for a backup.

The next three statements take the existing formats from the SAS catalog and copy them to SAS Viya using PROC FORMAT. The casfmtlib name (in the example "carFormats") can be anything you want. It helps to make it meaningful and related to the formats it contains but you can follow whatever naming convention you wish.

Finally, the SAS Viya format library is promoted to global scope and the backup copy is made. SAS Viya allows format libraries to have either SESSION or GLOBAL scope. By default, when created, all format libraries have session scope. This means that the formats are available to all actions in the current session (remember we created a CAS session at the start of this program?). When the session ends, the formats are no longer available. With global scope, the formats are available to all sessions for as long as the server is running. Since we want our formats to be available to anyone who tries to use the data, we need to make sure they have global scope. In CAS speak, this is done by promoting the formats from session to global scope. When loading the formats in either SAS Environment Manager or using the Command-Line Interface, this promotion to global scope is done for you.

After running this code, if you jump back over to SAS Environment Manager and choose User-Defined Formats, you will see that the format library carFormats is now defined and the formats it contains are available.

Display 17. Formats visible in SAS Environment Manager after loading using SAS Studio

If you are a SAS programmer, or typically create your data and formats using SAS programs, SAS Studio provides an environment for you to run your SAS code and also make the formats available to SAS Viya in a single program.

METHOD 3: SAS COMMAND-LINE INTERFACE

The final method described to load a format library to SAS Viya is arguably the easiest. The SAS Command-Line interface is included with SAS Viya and provides a direct process for calling the underlying services used by SAS Viya. No user interface, no programming environment, you just issue the commands directly at an operating system command. And while it is possible using the command-line interface to create formats, in the example here we will only take an existing SAS 9 catalog of formats and load them.

This is especially convenient if you want to load or update your formats as part of an automated process. A script that contains the commands could even be scheduled or included as part of a work flow.

How easy is it? Specify the URL for your system, log on, and issue a single command to load the formats.

This example uses the same format catalog as the previous two. This example is being run on Linux but the command-line interface is available on most hosts. The command-line interface is typically installed in this directory:

- /opt/sas/viya/home/bin

Navigate to that directory. The first thing you must do is create a profile to define the system that you want to access. Then log on. Once you have defined a profile, you can use it in subsequent sessions. Your session will last for a set period, typically a few hours, depending on your system settings.

The commands to create a profile and log on are:

- ./sas-admin profile init
- ./sas-admin auth login

These commands will prompt you to supply the necessary values. The Service Endpoint is the fully qualified URL for your system, including "http" or "https". The other values should be self-explanatory.

Once you have logged in successfully, a single command will take your format catalog as input and create a corresponding format library, also adding it to the existing search order:

- ./sas-admin cas format-libraries create –format-library <formatLibraryName> --server <serverName> --source-path <formatCatalogLocationOnDisk> --search-order <formatLibrarySearchOrder> --su

Supply the values for this command and you will get a message telling you the format library has been created and where it has been placed in the search order. A sample session showing the expected responses follows.

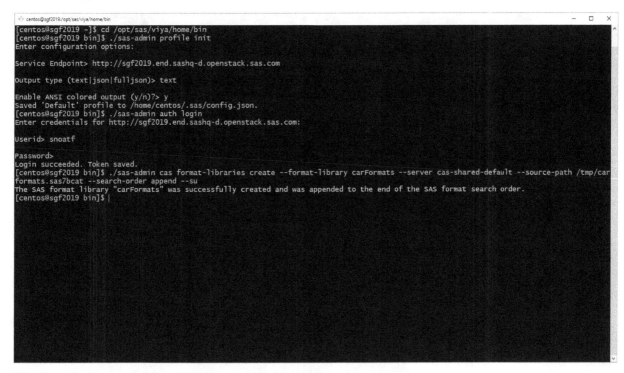

Display 17. Command line interface to load formats

To verify the results, check in SAS Environment Manager and you will see your new format library defined.

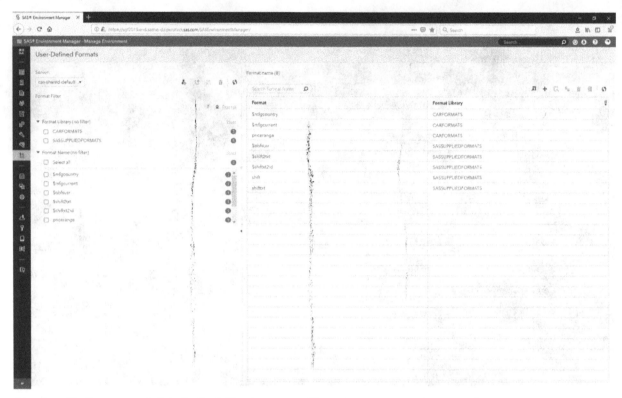

Display 17. Formats visible in SAS Environment Manager after loading using command line interface

It really is that easy. These commands can easily be included as part of a scripted process to load new formats on demand. And since it can be scripted, even a very large volume of format libraries can be loaded quickly using this process.

If you are comfortable using OS level commands and have direct access to a machine where the SAS Command Line Interface is installed, this is most likely the approach you will choose.

CONCLUSION

There are a number of different ways to take formats created in SAS 9 and make them available to SAS Visual Analytics on SAS Viya. Each has advantages and limitations and which you choose will be based on your specific requirements. The variety of options available should cover the needs for any situation.

All SAS code used in this paper is included as snippets in the References section in a format that enables easy cut and paste.

Documentation for SAS Formats, SAS Viya Administration, SAS Environment Manager, SAS Studio, and the SAS Command-Line Interface are all available online.

REFERENCES

- *Code snippet to create the formats used in this paper*

```
libname sgf2019 "/tmp/sgf2019" ;
proc format library=sgf2019.carFormats ;
    value $mfgCountry
            "Acura" = "Japan"
            "Audi" = "Germany"
            "BMW" = "Germany"
            "Buick" = "USA"
            "Cadillac" = "USA"
            "Chevrolet" = "USA"
            "Chrysler" = "USA"
            "Dodge" = "USA"
            "Ford" = "USA"
            "GMC" = "USA"
            "Honda" = "Japan"
            "Hyundai" = "Korea"
            "Infiniti" = "Japan"
            "Isuzu" = "Japan"
            "Jaguar" = "United Kingdom"
            "Jeep" = "USA"
            "Kia" = "Korea"
            "Land Rover" = "United Kingdom"
            "Lexus" = "Japan"
            "Lincoln" = "USA"
            "MINI" = "United Kingdom"
            "Mazda" = "Japan"
            "Mercedes-Benz" = "Germany"
            "Mercury" = "USA"
            "Mitsubishi" = "Japan"
            "Nissan" = "Japan"
            "Oldsmobile" = "USA"
            "Pontiac" = "USA"
            "Porsche" = "Germany"
            "Saab" = "Sweden"
            "Saturn" = "USA"
            "Scion" = "Japan"
            "Subaru" = "Japan"
            "Suzuki" = "Japan"
            "Toyota" = "Japan"
            "Volkswagen" = "Germany"
            "Volvo" = "Sweden"
            other = "_unknown_"
    ;

    value $mfgCurrent
            "Isuzu" = "No"
            "Mercury" = "No"
            "Oldsmobile" = "No"
            "Pontiac" = "No"
            "Saab" = "No"
            "Saturn" = "No"
```

22

```
        "Suzuki" = "No"
        other = "Yes"
   ;

   value priceRange
        0-15000 = "Budget"
        15001-30000 = "Medium"
        30001-40000 = "High"
        other = "Luxury"
   ;
run ;
```

- *Code snippet to create the data used in this paper*

```
options fmtsearch=(SGF2019.carFormats) ;

data sgf2019.carData (keep=make model mfgCountry type MSRP msrp_range mpg
mfgAvail) ;
    attrib make length=$13
    model length=$40
    type length=$8
    mfgCountry length=$32 format=$mfgCountry. label="Country of origin"
    mfgAvail length=$32 format=$mfgCurrent. label="Available in US?"
    mpg length=8. format=4.1 label="Combined city/hwy mileage"
    MSRP length=8. format=DOLLAR8. label="Suggested Retail Price in USD"
    msrp_range length=8. format=priceRange. label="Price Range"
    ;
    set sashelp.cars (keep=make model type MSRP mpg_city mpg_highway) ;
    mfgCountry = make ;
    msrp_range = MSRP ;
    mfgAvail = make ;
    mpg = ((.55*mpg_city) + (.45*mpg_highway)) ;
run ;
```

- *Code snippet to load the formats using SAS Studio*

```
/* create a cas session */
cas udfSession sessopts=(caslib=casuser timeout=1800 locale="en_US");

/* assign all the cas libraries */
caslib _all_ assign;

/* Identify format catalogs to move to server */
catname work.mycat(sgf2019.carFormats) ;

/* Collect formats in work.temp */
proc format
    library=work.mycat
    cntlout=temp;
run;
```

```
/* Move the format library from SAS Client to Cas session. */
proc format cntlin=temp sessref=udfSession
    casfmtlib='carFormats';
run ;

/* Promote the format library to global scope */
cas udfSession promotefmtlib fmtlibname=carFormats replace;

/* Save the format library to a table */
cas udfSession savefmtlib fmtlibname=carFormats caslib=Formats
table=carformats replace;
```

- *Code snippet to load the formats using the command line interface*

```
cd /opt/sas/viya/home/bin
./sas-admin profile init
./sas-admin auth login
./sas-admin cas format-libraries create --format-library carFormats --
server cas-shared-default --source-path /tmp/carformats.sas7bvat --search-
order append -su
```

ACKNOWLEDGMENTS

Rick Langston and Denise Poll of SAS deserve the credit for SAS Formats, the FORMAT Procedure, and the process for making formats available in SAS Viya.

Additional work, including making the command-line interface available, was done by Jeff Schrilla and James Holman, also from SAS.

Mark Fulp of SAS implemented the User-Defined Formats section of SAS Environment Manager.

CONTACT INFORMATION

Your comments and questions are valued and encouraged. Contact the author at:

Andrew Fagan
SAS
Andrew.Fagan@sas.com

SAS and all other SAS Institute Inc. product or service names are registered trademarks or trademarks of SAS Institute Inc. in the USA and other countries. ® indicates USA registration.

Other brand and product names are trademarks of their respective companies.

Check out these related books in the SAS® bookstore:

For 20% off these e-books, visit **sas.com\books** and use the code WITHSAS20

www.ingramcontent.com/pod-product-compliance
Lightning Source LLC
Chambersburg PA
CBHW080535060326
40690CB00022B/5141